KNITS THAT FIT

KNITS THAT FIT

INSTRUCTIONS, PATTERNS, AND TIPS FOR GETTING THE RIGHT FIT

edited by Potter Craft

POTTER
CRAFT

NEW YORK

CONTENTS

preface

A handknit sweater shouldn't fit like something that came from a department store. When you lovingly labor over a garment stitch-by-stitch, you want it to fit to your actual measurements, not just a general size. This volume offers you the chance to break free from following a pattern word-for-word and learn how to tailor your knitwear perfectly.

Featuring the best of Potter Craft, this volume brings together patterns from beloved designers Melissa Matthay, Sally Melville, Caddy Melville Ledbetter, Annie Modesitt, and Berta Karapetyan. From classic pullovers and cardigans to sexy tank tops and stylish cover-ups, there's something to knit for every occasion.

Additionally, you'll find tips and techniques from fitting experts Sally Melville, Amy Singer, and Jillian Moreno, who show you how to tweak nearly any pattern to better fit your unique shape. Whatever your size, shape, or style, with the measuring and fitting techniques presented here, you'll find it easy to create your perfect fit. Stop following, and start knitting!

Opposite page: a variation of the Classic Shirt (page 81).

chapter one

FIT BASICS

Knitting for You: One of the toughest things for any knitter to come to terms with is the knitting pattern. If you're like most knitters, you assume that since somebody wrote and published a pattern, and some of your friends have already knit it, the same pattern must work for you, right?

Wrong! Knitting a pattern without making any modifications is one of the biggest mistakes knitters make. Chances are, any given pattern isn't designed for your body (unless you're best friends with the designer!) any more than a finished sweater from the store is. But the good news is that unlike a store-bought item, which would need tailoring to modify its shape and style, knitting a customized garment requires some forethought and math to adjust the pattern to create a garment that will fit just the way you want it to. In this chapter, we present the ins and outs of measuring and modifying a pattern.

■ *CONTRIBUTED BY Sally Melville, Jillian Moreno, and Amy R. Singer*

KNIT TO FIT

The odds that a pattern will fit you (or the person the project is intended to fit) perfectly as designed are slim to none. In fact, every pattern contains directions that you should never follow blindly. Although knitting patterns usually don't tell you exactly where to "edit," you should be able to apply the modifications by Sally Melville in the following sections to most patterns.

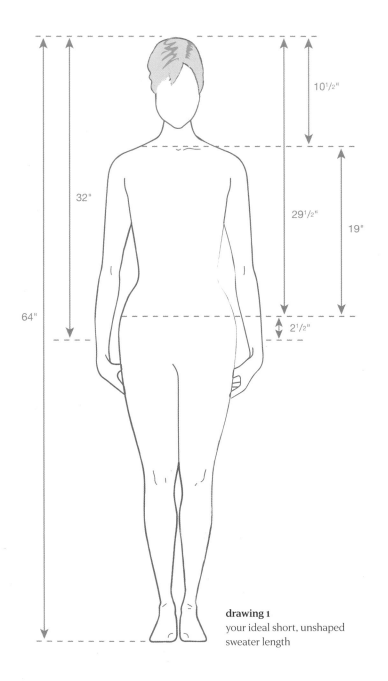

drawing 1
your ideal short, unshaped
sweater length

Common Customizations

There are five places where individual fit should override a pattern:

- finished garment length
- waist length (if the garment has waist shaping)
- sleeve length (if the garment has sleeves)
- number of stitches in the cuff (if the garment is tight at the wrist)
- shoulder width (if the garment has shoulder definition)

Directions for all these measurements and changes are listed in the following sections. Remember that any changes to the original pattern may change the yardage of materials required, so adjust the quantities appropriately.

Getting Real

Who exactly are you knitting for? If the answer is you, the first step is both the easiest and the hardest of them all: Look in the mirror. Like it or not (hopefully you like it!), that image is your customer. That's who you're knitting for! You aren't knitting for the body you had ten years ago, or will have in just six months if you stay on that diet. (**Note:** Even though we assume that you're knitting for yourself in this book, the instructions will help you figure out how to customize a pattern for any intended recipient by taking just a few measurements.)

Just as important, you aren't knitting the size tag from your favorite top. Sizes vary widely from company to company and over time. The same brand you love probably has a different size 8 now than it did eight years ago! The only way to get the results you want is to make sure you're knitting for the one and only reflection staring back at you.

OK, so let's get started. The following pages address all the ins and outs of measuring you, but there's one companion you should bring with you on your measuring journey: your favorite sweater of the

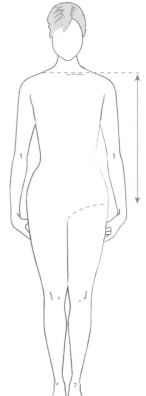

drawing a
your ideal midlength

same style you are about to knit. It's your favorite for a reason: It fits the way you like it to! So as you measure your own lengths and widths, you should take the basic measurements of your sweater as well. They'll help you determine at least one of your ideal sweater lengths and your preferred ease, or the difference between your measurements and the garment's measurements. (For more on ease, see page **14**.)

Measure Up: Lengths

When it comes to how long your sweaters or tops should be, we defer to expert knitter Sally Melville, the queen of fit and flatter. For more on her philosophy, see page **16**. If you have your own favorite lengths, feel free to adjust the information below as needed.

Get your tape measure ready!

Sweater Length
Short

The hem of a short sweater, whether shaped (knit to follow the contours of the body) or unshaped, should fall somewhere between the waist and the hips.
Measure your height in inches [centimeters].

Divide this measurement by 2.

Subtract 2½" [6.5cm].

Place a small book (or something else that's flat) on top of your head. Have a friend measure from the top of your head to the top of your shoulder, above your collarbone. This is your head and neck

measurement. (**Note:** If you're alone, use a ruler and a pencil to make marks on the wall at the top of your head and your shoulder; just make sure to do it a couple of times to verify the accuracy.)

Subtract the head and neck measurement from half your height minus 2½" [6.5cm].

Because you're not a straight line, and curves will ultimately subtract from the length, use the Sizing Chart on page **140** to make the following adjustments to compensate for any extra girth:

- If you knit size XS, do nothing.
- If you knit size S, add ½" [13mm].
- If you knit size M, add 1" [2.5cm]
- If you knit size L, add 1½" [3.8cm].
- If you knit size 1X, add 2" [5cm].
- If you knit size 2X, add 2½" [6.5cm].
- For larger sizes, add 2½" [6.5cm] plus ½" [13mm] per additional size.

This measurement is your ideal length for an unshaped Short Sweater (drawing 1).

To calculate the length of a shaped Short Sweater, you have a choice: It could be either the same length as an unshaped one, or slightly longer. Read what follows about midlength, which refers to ideal lengths for shaped sweaters.

Midlength

Any sweater with a hem that hits at the hips is a Midlength Sweater.
Because Midlength Sweaters look best if they fall at the widest part of the hip, and because this point usually is close to hwwalf of a person's height, you may simply add 2½" [6.5cm] to your ideal Short Sweater length. (You're adding back the 2½" [6.5cm] that were subtracted in the Short Sweater calculations.)

But the widest part of your hip may not fall at half your height, and can vary depending on the pants you wear. Double-check this measurement with the following exercise while wearing the pants you would wear with the sweater.

Standing straight (again, against a wall if it helps), hold the tape measure at the top of one shoulder, above the collarbone. Unfurl the tape measure, letting it ride over the bust and down your leg to the floor. Find the measurement where the tape measure meets the widest part of your hip, as revealed by the pants you are wearing.

This measurement is your ideal length for a Midlength Sweater (drawing 2).

Long

Any sweater with a hem that hits below the hips is a Long Sweater.

Put on a pair of pants or tights that you would wear with your long sweater. First, looking in the mirror, find the place where you'd like the hem to fall to create a slim silhouette. You'll likely want it to fall below the point where your legs widen to your hip; where, exactly, is up to you. Be sure to consider where it falls from the back view, too!

Again, standing straight, hold the tape measure at the top of one shoulder, above the collarbone, and unfurl the tape measure; measure to the point that you've identified in the mirror.

This measurement is your ideal length for a Long Sweater (drawing 3).

Back Waist Length

This measurement applies only to garments with waist shaping.

To find your Back Waist length, start by locating the bone that sticks out the most at the base of your neck. Have a friend measure from this bone down your back and to your waist. (To find your waist, hold your index finger at the point where your back "breaks" when you lean backward.)

This measurement is your Back Waist length (drawing 4).

You may want the garment's waist to be at your natural waist, or 1"-2" [2.5cm-5cm] higher than your natural waistline to create a long-legged look.

To Change a Pattern's Finished Garment Length:
You'll find the Finished Garment length for any top in the measurements or schematics of the pattern. If the Finished Garment measurement is different from your ideal measurement, all you have to do is add or subtract the difference. Changing length in sweaters with no waist shaping simply means working fewer or more rows. But if the garment is shaped at the waist, changing length may mean working fewer or more rows between the increases or decreases that produce the shaping. Some patterns may tell you where to lengthen or shorten. But for those that don't, here are the guidelines.

- In garments with no armhole or waist shaping, change Finished Garment length anywhere between the hem and the neck.
- In garments with armhole shaping, change Finished Garment length between the hem and the armhole. (The armhole depth is particular to the size of the sleeve and shouldn't be changed.)
- In garments with waist shaping, adjust the Finished Garment length between the hem and the waist, and the Back Waist length between the waist and armhole.

Here's an example: You want to knit a Midlength Sweater (page **11**) with waist shaping, and the pattern's Back Waist length is 16" [40.5cm], but yours is 17" [43cm], and the pattern's Finished Garment length is 22" [56cm], which is the same as yours. The pattern will instruct you to shorten or lengthen for the Back Waist length between the waist and the armhole; you'll insert more rows to add 1" [2.5cm] of length. But then you will have added 1" [2.5cm] to the Finished Garment length as well. So, where the pattern tells you to shorten or lengthen between the hem and waist shaping, work fewer rows to subtract 1" [2.5cm] from the total length.

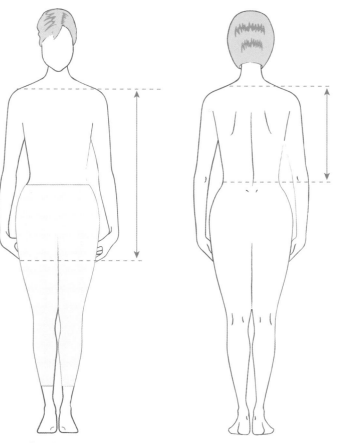

drawing 3
your ideal long
sweater length

drawing 4
your back waist length

Sleeve Length

Sleeve length is a tailoring term that measures from the center of the neck to the cuff (or hem) of the sleeve—usually, to the wrist. (It's measured this way so this one measurement can apply to all styles of sweaters, with drop-shoulder, saddle, raglan, or set-in sleeves.) And just as with Finished Garment length, you first need to measure to find your ideal Sleeve length.

Stand with your arm bent 90 degrees at the elbow, and have a friend measure from the center of the base of your neck, across your shoulders, and around your curved arm to the wrist. (**Note:** If you prefer shorter sleeves than in the pattern, simply measure to the point where you'd like to have the sleeves end.)

This measurement is your ideal Sleeve length (drawing 5).

This measurement will be appropriate for lightweight sweaters and other garments with a tight upper arm. But heavy, loosely knit fabrics can stretch, making the sleeves too long with this measurement. For them, you might want to knit the sleeves 1" [2.5cm] shorter than your ideal Sleeve length.

For a loose sleeve that blouses above a snug cuff, you may need to add 1" [2.5cm] to the total sleeve length to accommodate the extra material required for the upper arm.

Because many patterns don't give finished Sleeve lengths, here's how to figure them out.

- Determine the width of the garment between the top of the sleeves, and divide that measurement by two.
- Find the length of the sleeve.
- Add these two numbers to find the total Sleeve length for the garment.

To Change a Pattern's Sleeve Length:

Find the difference between your ideal Sleeve length and the Finished Garment length.

To shorten (or lengthen) the sleeve, work fewer (or more) rows as follows:

- In garments without armhole shaping (e.g., a drop-shoulder sleeve), change the length anywhere between the cast-on and final bind-off.
- In garments with armhole shaping (e.g., set-in or raglan sleeves), change the length before the armhole shaping.

You may also shorten (or lengthen) by working fewer (or more) rows between the increases that shape the sleeve.

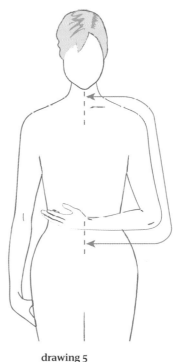

drawing 5
your sleeve length

Measure Up: Widths

No matter how hard you work to get the length just right, without careful attention to the width, your garment may still fail to flatter. In fact, garment width is what most people think of first when they think of fit, for good reason. But everyone has their own ideal fit when it comes to how tight or loose a top fits—there are so many different body types and different tastes that it is impossible to find a universally flattering formula for ideal widths as for length.

That said, once you figure out a few measurements and what you like, changing the width of a garment is just as easy as changing its length.

Bust, Waist, and Hips

Unlike garment sizes, which have changed greatly over the last few decades, the three standard measurements you need to customize your knitting haven't changed at all. Chances are that you already know what they are, but just in case you don't: They're the Bust, Waist, and Hips. When you're taking these measurements, use the same tape measure for all three so they're consistent.

The Bust is the most problematic of these three measurements. *It isn't your bra size!* Measure your circumference over the widest part of your breasts (usually at the nipples) and around your back. Before measuring, be sure to put on your best sweater bra and a tight tank or T-shirt. And remember: *Don't hold your breath!*

The Waist measurement is more of a personal preference. You can measure a bit higher or lower than your actual waist if your favorite tops are the ones that tend to "fake" a higher or lower waist.

The Hips measurement is easy to take—around the widest part of your hips—but tempting to round down. *Don't do it!* Cheating your measurement here (or anywhere else) will only cheat you out of a good fit. For maximum accuracy, wear leggings or tight-fitting yoga pants.

Now for the really good news: After you've taken just those three measurements, you'll have 90 percent of the information you need to get the right fit from your knitting patterns.

Ease

The other 10 percent of the information needed to create knits that fit comes from that magic E word: ease. Put simply, *ease* is the amount of space between you and your garment—that is, the difference between your standard measurements and the measurements of the garment. So if your bust measures 38" [96.5cm]

and the finished bust measurement for the garment you're about to knit is 42" [106.5cm], the garment will have 4" [10cm] of ease. If you want a snugger fit around the bust, knit a smaller size.

There is also what's called negative ease. *Negative ease* is when the garment's measurements are actually smaller than your own, and the fabric must stretch to cover you.

Here are some common kinds of ease, defined by changes from the chest (or bust) measurement.

- Very Tight: Less than the actual measurement, to -2" [-5cm].
- Very Close Fitting: 0" [0cm] (no ease).
- Close Fitting: +0"-2" [2.5cm-5cm].
- Standard Fitting: +2" cm-4" [5cm-10cm].
- Loose Fitting: +4" cm-6" [10cm-15cm].
- Oversized: More than 6" [15cm].

Sometimes we find that the amount of ease we want is between two sizes. (Remember that you always want to take measurements from that garment of a matching style and weight and compare it with the schematic of the garment you are knitting.) The solution might be to combine sizes offered by the pattern. Here's what you could do.

- Divide the finished bust measurement of the larger size by 2.
- Divide the finished bust measurement of the smaller size by 2.
- Add these two numbers together: did this give you the finished measurement you want?
- If so, then work the larger size for the Front and the smaller size for the Back.
- For some styles, you will need to decide on which Sleeve size you are making. Make the armhole depths match the size Sleeve you are making.
- Do not change the neck (which is usually the same for all sizes).
- You might find you need to wiggle the numbers at the shoulders so your shoulder seams match.

One last note on ease: A garment with ease will drape on your curves. Ease is affected by the shape of the garment, the shape of your body, and the yarn used to create the fabric. A garment knit in a thick, heavy yarn generally requires more ease to drape in a flattering way than the same pattern knit in a thin, lightweight yarn.

Shoulder Width

Shoulder width is the last piece of the puzzle. It isn't a contour measurement, like the Big 3, but it's just as important to consider before you start knitting a garment. The edge-to-edge measurement across the piece of a garment with shoulder definition is the *Shoulder width*. (**Note:** This measurement doesn't apply to drop-shoulder or raglan styles but does apply to those with set-in sleeves or shoulder straps as well as to sleeveless garments.)

Shoulder width is an important measurement because it can vary from your actual "size." For instance, you may be a size Small with wider-than-average shoulders or a well-endowed woman with narrow shoulders. No matter what the case may be, the Shoulder width of your finished garment should fit your body. Here's how to find it.

Put on a garment with set-in sleeves that fits you well and has shoulder seams, and have a friend measure the distance between the seams across your back. (**Note:** If you don't own such a garment, have your friend measure between where you would like the seams to be.)

This measurement is your ideal Shoulder width (drawing 6).

It can be used as is, or you may want to increase or decrease it by 1" [2.5cm], depending on the garment. For example,

- You may feel that a vest would look more flattering if the shoulder width between the armholes was 1" [2.5cm] wider than your actual shoulder width.
- A garment with straps might be as much as 3" [7.5cm] narrower.
- In a garment with sleeves, especially if the yarn is heavy and the upper arm is full, the sleeves could pull the garment off your shoulders, so you might narrow the measurement by 1" [2.5cm].

To Change a Pattern's Shoulder Width:

Find the finished Shoulder width (in the finished measurements or schematics). If it's different from your measurement, adjust the "Shape Armhole" directions as follows.

Multiply the stitches per inch [centimeter] by your Shoulder width. Round it to a whole number, odd or even, as suits the pattern. Add 2 stitches if needed for seams.

The resulting number is the ideal number of stitches in your Shoulder width.

Bind off as directed at the underarm.

When decreasing to Shoulder width, work more or fewer decreases to attain the stitches of your Shoulder width. (For small sizes, you might have to increase to your Shoulder width. Do this gradually as you approach the shoulder.)

You'll have different numbers of stitches for all of the pattern's subsequent directions. Don't change the neck numbers; absorb your changes into the shoulder instructions. (For example, if you have 4 fewer stitches for the Shoulder width, bind off 2 fewer stitches than directed for each shoulder.)

drawing 6
your shoulder width

MAKING THE MOST OF YOUR SWEATER'S SHAPE

Even when you have knitted a beautiful garment that fits and flatters, you can ruin the overall look by wearing it with the wrong thing! So how can you ensure that what you make always presents beautifully? It's all based on the concepts of proportion (i.e., lengths and styles) and shape (i.e., what you wear with what), and Sally Melville's guidelines that follow will help you solve almost any wardrobe dilemma.

drawing 7
the hourglass figure

Achieving a Natural Hourglass Shape

The archetype of the female shape is the hourglass—larger bust and hips with an emphasized slimness between. Whatever your shape and whatever your age, it's some version of the hourglass that you often wish to attain. To interpret an hourglass shape, you would wear a top that appears to narrow between the bust and waist with a bottom garment that continues the hourglass over the lower half of your body. Achieving this shape with knitted garments requires attention to length and shape, then styling.

Garment Length and Shape
Short Sweaters
Suppose you want to wear an unshaped Short Sweater. Can it suggest an hourglass shape? Absolutely! For most people, the waist is narrower than the bust and hips, so a Short Sweater that sits well above the hips will allow the world to see the torso narrowing toward a waist. (The Short Sweater would be the top part of the hourglass, and the exposed near-waist area would be the center of the hourglass.)

But where should a Short Sweater fall? Two pieces of information are helpful here. First, something that isn't cut precisely in half is more visually interesting than something that's cut right across its middle. And second, I believe that there's a place on the body—slightly higher than the midpoint between the feet and the top of the head—that puts the upper and lower body into an attractive balance. This formula is given in the previous section as your ideal length for a Short Sweater (page **11**).

The ideal length for a Short Sweater gives a slightly long-legged silhouette and exposes just the right amount of midsection to show the hips narrowing to the waist (drawing 8). On most people, the hem will be near the center of the belly, effectively cutting the belly

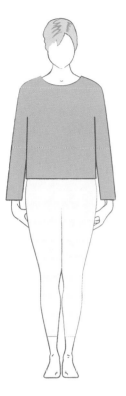

drawing 8
an unshaped sweater
at ideal short length

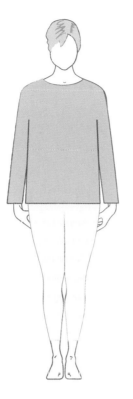

drawing 9
an unshaped
midlength sweater

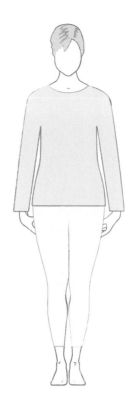

drawing 10
a shaped sweater
at ideal midlength

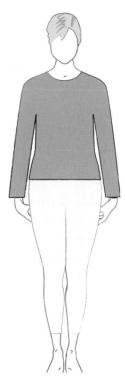

drawing 11
a shaped sweater
at ideal short length

in half, which is good news—because one of the best ways to make something look smaller is to cut it in half. (**Note:** If the sweater is shorter than this ideal length, your legs will look longer, but more of the midsection—perhaps more than you'd like!—will be exposed; if the sweater is longer—say, to the midpoint between your head and the floor—your legs will look shorter, you will look top-heavy, and, more important, the middle of the hourglass won't be visible.)

Midlength Sweaters
Can you also achieve the hourglass shape with a Midlength Sweater? Absolutely! But the sweater must be shaped. An unshaped Midlength Sweater says, "This is how wide I am at my hips, and I continue at this width to my bust!" The resulting silhouette is a wide rectangle—not the shape that most people wish to present to the world (drawing 9).

A Midlength Sweater needs visible narrowing at the waist to define the center of the hourglass (drawing 10). By the way, waist shaping does not demand that the shaping sit precisely at the actual waist;

slightly higher waist shaping can create a flattering interpretation of the hourglass. Nor does waist shaping need to hug your actual waist; often the suggestion of a waist is enough. (So, although your waistline might be 8" [20.5cm] narrower than your bust, successful sweater shapes might narrow only 4" [10cm] at the waist.)

The natural place for the hem of a shaped Midlength Sweater is at the widest part of the hips, which will, on many people, approach the midpoint of the body (i.e., halfway between the head and the floor). (**Note:** This formula appears in the previous section as your ideal length for a Midlength Sweater.)

You might ask why the ideal Short Sweater length wasn't used for this sweater. Well, it could be (drawing 11). And you actually might prefer a shorter length for wearing with a skirt, whereas it might look a little short with pants. And compare drawing 11 with drawing 10: Don't the hips—divided in half in drawing 10—look narrower? (Remember, one of the best ways to narrow something is to divide it in half.) Here you have a choice.

drawing 12
a shaped sweater
at ideal long length

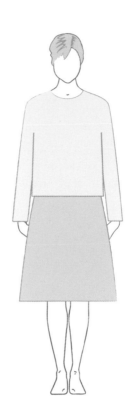

drawing 13
a short, unshaped, sweater
and an A-line skirt

drawing 14
an unshaped, cropped
sweater and a longer top

Long Sweaters

And what of the Long Sweater that you love? Can it define the hourglass shape? Of course it can, if it has waist shaping (drawing 12).

There's no ideal length for a shaped Long Sweater; its length will be your personal preference. Your ideal length for a Long Sweater might depend on your height: Because long garments make you look shorter, a tall person might want a longer sweater, and vice versa. It might depend on your shape: If you have ample thighs, you might prefer to cover more of them. And it might depend on the style of the garment: Do you want to wear the sweater as a dress?

What You Wear with It

When putting together an outfit, you may pay more attention to the colors than to the shapes or fabrics of the garments. And it's sad when the effect of a beautiful garment is ruined by styling. For example, an unshaped Short Sweater might not look good with slim pants: If your hips are wide, you may look bottom heavy; if your hips are narrow, you may look top heavy. Make sure that the rest of your outfit complements the hourglass shape started by the sweater's silhouette.

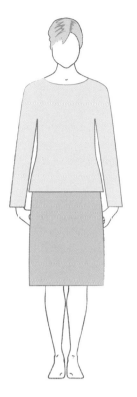

drawing 15
a shaped, mid-length sweater
and a straight skirt

drawing 16
a shaped, mid-length
sweater and slim pants

With an Unshaped Short Sweater:

If you like your hips, continue the hourglass look with straight pants. But I personally don't love this silhouette; not much of the feminine hourglass shows through. My preference is to pair an unshaped Short Sweater with an A-line skirt (drawing 13). (**Note:** I use the the term *A-line* loosely; look for skirts that fit smoothly at the waist and float over the hips.)

If your Short Sweater is cropped—that is, shorter than your ideal length for a Short Sweater (see page 11)—you might wear an accessory that ends at your ideal length for a Short Sweater (drawing 14). The accessory could be a belt or a tight top, either of which would emphasize the slimness exposed by the cropped sweater.

With a Shaped Midlength Sweater:

Pair a Midlength Sweater (page 11) with a straight or slim bottom (pants or skirt). (**Note:** A straight fit is one that hugs the hips and continues straight toward the floor without tapering, and a slim fit narrows from hip to knee and then continues straight toward to the floor.) Just make sure that the sweater ends at the widest part of the hip as revealed by your bottom garment (drawing 15).

I think a Midlength Sweater looks too long when worn with an A-line skirt; a shaped Short Sweater might be preferable in this instance.

With a Shaped Long Sweater:

The length of your Long Sweater should complement your body shape. Wear your Long Sweater with slim pants, leggings, or tights. The longer the garment, the less of the thigh exposed. Choose a lighter-weight leg covering with a longer Long Sweater and a heavier-weight leg covering with a shorter Long Sweater. All of these choices might be leg coverings you would never wear unless the shapelier parts of your middle were covered (drawing 16)!

Layering (Real or Imagined)

At this point, it may seem that the best way to style your wardrobe is to match Short Sweaters with skirts and Midlength Sweaters with pants. But you want more choices, don't you? Layering is almost always the right answer.

An unshaped Short Sweater looks beautiful with pants when it's worn over a shaped Midlength Sweater. And a shaped Midlength Sweater with an A-line skirt doesn't look too long if it has "imagined layering" created with a change of color or yarn or stitch pattern at the waist.

OTHER DESIRABLE SHAPES AND HOW TO ACHIEVE THEM

Now you've learned how to achieve the illusion of a natural hourglass shape. But what about other shapes? Wouldn't life be dull—and style severely limited—if what you wear could only be drawn to this one, tightly prescribed silhouette? And truly, some days you just don't feel like an hourglass and don't want to make any attempt to look like one. You just want to put on a big, long sweater and head out to the cottage or the grocery store or to walk the dog. Can you still look good? Of course! In fact, these sweaters can take you into high fashion! All you need to do is reexamine your assumptions about length, shape, and styling.

Slim Rectangle

When you wear big, long sweaters with no waist shaping, you forgo the hourglass shape. But what's the next-best thing to the hourglass, a style that's occasionally been the epitome of female beauty? The slim rectangle! Because the eye extends what it sees (and won't imagine what it can't see), ideally, you want a long sweater to fall to a slim part of the body. The eye will then extend this slimness upward—no hips, no butt, no belly—making the body appear as a slim rectangle. This slimmest point is somewhere below the widest point of the hips.

A big, long sweater also needs to have enough ease built into it that there's no suggestion of the body parts that are being deemphasized. You could produce a big, long, and unshaped sweater that is generous

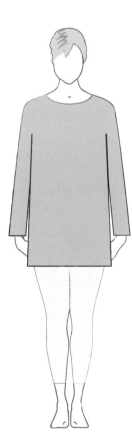

drawing 17
a long, unshaped sweater

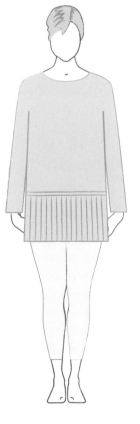

drawing 18
a long, unshaped sweater and short sweater line

drawing 19
a long, unshaped sweater and vest

from top to bottom—say, hips +6" (15cm) or more (drawing 17). While they hang loose and free, these comfy sweaters do run the risk of looking like a sack. One way to improve the style is to add some sort of demarcation (a different color, yarn, or stitch pattern) at your ideal length for a Short Sweater (drawing 18). Or, you could wear a vest to this length (drawing 19). Both these choices will make the outfit more interesting and make you look taller.

A-Line

Another way to draw a fabulous silhouette (my personal favorite) is to make big sweaters generous at the hip only—that is, big, long, and A-line (drawing 20). Because its extra-generous hem makes the hip look slim in comparison and then describes an upwardly narrowing silhouette, this shape needn't cover as

much of the leg; it may be worn shorter, at just above crotch length. And this is good, because anything that exposes the full length of the leg makes the body look taller.

What You Wear with It

You want to wear a long sweater with something slim enough to show the narrowness of the leg—the template for the desired shape.

With an Unshaped Long Sweater:
- Knit it to fall to a slim part of the leg.
- Wear it with slim pants, leggings, or tights. (The same suggestions hold true here as for styling a long, shaped sweater in the section above.)

With an A-Line Long Sweater:
- Knit it to the leg break (where the leg meets the hip) or longer.
- Wear it with slim or straight pants or a slim or straight skirt.

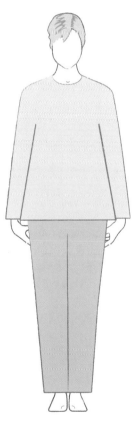

drawing 20
a long, A-line sweater
with straight pants

YARN TIPS FOR A BETTER FIT

Now that you've measured yourself, it's time to talk yarn. From gauge to color to texture, there's a lot to consider. Take these tips, adapted from Jillian Moreno and Amy R. Singer, the next time you go yarn shopping to find the most flattering yarn for your sweater's shape.

Think Like a Sewer

When fashion designers and home sewers choose their fabrics, they do so carefully. They know that not only the color and pattern but also the texture of a fabric will be crucial as to how the finished garment looks when worn. If you think about your favorite dress, for example, you probably could describe the material—how it feels, how it drapes, and how it looks on you. But for some reason, if you let knitters loose in a yarn store, they buy yarns on the basis of how appealing they are to the eye and the hand, not how they will act—or look—when knitted up into a garment. There's nothing wrong with buying yarns you like, but make sure you match them with the right project when the time comes.

Below are some guidelines on yarn texture and color that work best for knitted tops.

Fine Yarn for Fine Sweaters

Bulky yarn is every time-crunched knitter's friend. It knits up so quick! But bulky yarn's name says it all: It adds bulk. A thick yarn will never create a finished garment that drapes nicely, so unless you're extremely skinny and knitting a garment with negative ease, just use that chunky yarn for a scarf instead. Overly textured, fringed, fuzzy, or any other sort of novelty yarn also should be in the "not for a sweater" category. Sometimes they can work effectively as an accent or a trim, but chances are that a yarn with too much personality used throughout a sweater won't result in a sweater you love.

There's a reason most store-bought knitwear is knit at a superfine gauge: The finer the yarn, the sleeker the resulting garment and the better it will fit and drape. But save yourself a two-year project and don't go for superfine yarn, either, if you're hand-knitting. Look for the finest-gauge yarn that you can use and still stay sane. DK or worsted-weight yarns should work just fine, but any yarn that knits up 4 stitches to 1" [2.5cm] or finer is a great candidate for most knitters and most sweaters. They result in sweaters that fit and drape instead of puff up and block.

Color

Like fit, certain colors and motifs work best for different body types. Thinking about color the same way you think about shaping will significantly affect the wearability of your finished piece. What's the trick to using color in a way that tricks the eye? As with shaping and fitting your sweater, it's all about balance. Keep your body shape in mind, and you won't go wrong. The following tips should help.

Advancing and Receding

Entire books are devoted to color and colorwork, and with good reason: There's a lot of material to cover! But we're concerned with color only as it relates to fit. At the core of color and fit are the same principles you might have learned in an art class, because your eyes evaluate the colors of a garment the same way that they evaluate the colors in a painting.

Let's review a few of the most important things about the way color is perceived. First—and most important in a sweater—dark colors recede and light colors advance. That means if you want to downplay a certain part of your body, make sure you're not using a gradient yarn that will fade lighter over that specific part of your body. This principle works only to a degree, though; if you're knitting an XXL sweater, using black won't make it appear XS.

Almost as important as the difference between light and dark is the difference between warm and cool. Blues and other cool colors recede (like dark colors) whereas warm colors like red will be dominant and advance; they'll receive attention before the cool colors do. Contrast works the same way. If you're switching from red to blue, for example, the line where the color changes will draw more attention than if the yarn changed from one shade of blue to another.

Transitions

The transition between colors can be eye-catching or not, depending on how abrupt the transition appears, so use your gradients and your abrupt changes wisely! For example, if you want to downplay your belly, make sure to fade from a lighter (or warmer) yarn up top to a darker (or cooler) yarn down over your belly. If the change is abrupt, make sure it's not at the widest part of your body, which will draw more attention to a place where you least want it.

Speaking of abrupt changes in color, what about stripes? Chances are, you already know that horizontal stripes always make you look wider than you are. This rule also applies to self-striping yarns, which, although pretty, can create stripes across the body of a sweater.

Don't worry, though; you can use stripes and self-striping yarns in a smart way. A 2x2 slip stitch can create narrow stripes that read vertical, or you can knit from cuff to cuff so that the horizontal lines are turned vertical. Or, you can choose a self-striping yarn with a very gradual color changes that fade over the entire length of the sweater.

Texture

True, overly fuzzy or fringy yarn isn't something you want all over a sweater. But many other options can create texture, and many can enhance fit! When properly planned, texture can add pattern or physical lines that create a rhythm. Just keep in mind that adding texture can create a thicker, stiffer fabric, so the garment may need more shaping and less ease to ensure a good fit.

Knit and Purl

The most basic and satisfying way to add texture to a sweater is by varying knit and purl stitches. Knitting a swatch of the pattern you're considering will give you a good idea of whether you should use it all over or only on part of the sweater. Just be mindful of creating large horizontal bands of texture as you incorporate the stitch pattern into the sweater!

Ribbing

Ribbing is another easy way to add texture, and it can be a great fit-enhancing feature. It can be made in an almost infinite number of patterns (1x1, 2x2, and 3x1 ribs are just three examples), goes nicely with nearly any type of sweater, and is a great way to "fake" shaping. Although ribbing that is too tight can stretch and create a weird geometric effect, ribbing that skims the body pulls in gently and adds natural-looking shaping. For instance, a band of ribbing around the waist or at the sides adds instant curves without the need for much math.

Cables

Cables add thickness and direction to a sweater at the same time. Aim to create vertical lines, and be mindful of how thick the cable will make the fabric of your finished sweater. Think curvy with your cables (to accentuate your curves), and to keep the finished sweater sleek, make any crossed cable repeats rather long—say, crossing every 10 rows rather than every 5 rows.

Lace

Lace is the lightest of textures and not at all hard to knit. It makes a great edging or trim too! Like knit and purl patterns, lace patterns should be swatched to make sure they'll work in your sweater. The only real drawback to lace is that it drapes and stretches differently from other types of stitches; even different lace patterns act differently. That means substituting lace into a pattern that doesn't call for it can be risky. But the more you work with lace, the better sense you'll have of how the finished fabric will look and feel.

TIPS (AND AN IMPORTANT LESSON) FOR BIGGER KNITTERS

Jillian Moreno and Amy R. Singer are the experts when it comes to knitting for larger sizes. Once you've mastered their B3 system and their ingenious method for knitting side panels, you can adapt virtually any pattern to fit.

You've Got Parts–We've Got 3 Bs

When you're a Big Girl knitting for your Big Girl self, it can make your brain hurt to imagine what might look superfine on your body. We make it easy breaking down the process into instructions for three key body bits: Bust, Waist, and Hips, which we call Boobs, Belly, and Butt—otherwise referred to as the B3.

One or two of your Bs might be bigger than the others, or maybe they're all bountiful. What parts do you like? What parts would you rather downplay? Looking good and feeling good in knitwear (or any clothing, for that matter) is all about balancing your overall silhouette. By using different sweater styles and shapes that work with your particular Bs, and avoiding the ones that work against them, you'll knit sweaters that look killer on you.

And by the way, we aren't fans of the age-old fatgirl trick of attempted camouflage. Tents, smocks, and caftans only make you look as big as all that extra fabric. And fat girls in black don't look thinner; they just look like fat girls wearing black. Instead, we suggest practical prestidigitation, just like a magician. Magicians specialize in redirection: "Look here, not there."

So here's how to use the B3 system. Look in the mirror. Which one of your Bs is biggest and most bodacious? Use the must-dos and tips for that B below to help you choose knitting patterns that will flatter you or improve an existing knitting pattern (like adding short rows if you're a Boob girl). If you want to play up or down more than one B, choose a suitable tip for each B.

But in the end, it's all about you. If we say "Show off your girls" and you don't want to, don't. If we say "Cover that tush" but you think it's your hot spot, well, rock it, baby! The B3 "rules" are more like guidelines that give you a place to start, but only you get to say what works for you. You won't get sent to the knitting principal's office if you don't play our way.

Tips for All Big Girls

- **Think skim.** Your finished sweater must skim your shape, outlining your curves—not be as loose as a circus tent or so tight that people can see what you had for breakfast. There's a wide and personal range between these two extremes, but it's your body and your sweater, so it's really up to you.
- **Celebrate your waist!** Nip in the waist of your garments a little, even if you think you don't have a waist. Even 1" [2.5cm] can make a huge difference! Waist shaping defines the waist you have; creates the waist you didn't think you had; and gives you a curvy, feminine, and tailored silhouette.
- **Cables and twists.** Huge rope cables are related to the long-and-lean kind and give your knitwear flattering vertical lines. But big cables get thick and bulky, adding literal feet to your literal frame.
- **Hyped on horizontals.** Horizontal motifs are hard for every B to work with. There's almost no way to avoid the fact that horizontal lines make you look wider.
- **Beware of motif mania.** A single large intarsia motif on the front is a huge (no pun intended) don't. You may think it's a shield to hide your body, but it's really a great big spotlight focusing attention on everything it covers.

Must-Dos for Each B
Boobs
- Show as much skin at your chest as you dare; if you're shy, at least let your collarbones peek out...collarbones are sexy.
- Add waist shaping so you don't just look round all over.

Belly

- Hems should hit 1-2" (2.5-5cm) below your biggest Belly bit.
- Use dramatic neckline, cuff, and hem treatments to direct attention where you'd rather have it.
- Yoke sweaters are great for Belly girls. The yoke adds visual interest up top to balance a beautiful belly.

Butt

- Sweaters should stop above or below your biggest Butt bulge...not right on it.
- Create gentle shaping at the waist, then flare out to below your Butt.

Does more than one of your Bs stand up and sing? You, my good woman, are a combo platter. The easiest way to balance your combo platter is to think about the B that doesn't stand out and put on a show there.

- Boobs and Butt? Waist yourself.
- Boobs and Belly? Rock the rump.
- Belly and Butt? Up, up, and away.
- All 3 Bs? Add the whisper of a waist and keep it smooth. The triple-B combo needs to think "skim" more than any other. Try just 1" [2.5cm] less ease than you usually use. Because you are seeking balance, emphasize what you want to show off with your choice of shape, color, and ease.

Get a Little on the Side!

Sometimes taking a different approach is the only way, especially when talking about color and texture on a Big Girl bod. Got your Bust, Waist, and Hip measurements (see page **27**)? Good! Get your calculator, and let's try a new adaptation!

Side panels add extra width to a garment in the easiest way possible. Simply put, they're pieces knitted separately (usually) and then sewn into a sweater's side seams. You can use them to make a sweater that is heavily textured or has complicated colorwork bigger without messing with texture or color charts for the front and back pieces. Side panels are a great way to customize not only the size but also the look of a sweater: You can create side panels in colors and textures different from the rest of the body. Side panels work in sweaters that already have waist shaping, or you can add panels with waist shaping to a plain rectangle sweater and make it really fit you!

The simplest side panels are straight rectangles that add a consistent amount of width to each part of the sweater below the armholes. They also can be worked in various other shapes to add different amounts of width in different areas.

- Hourglass-shaped panels do double duty by offering both extra width and waist shaping, adding more width at the Bust and Hip than at the Waist.
- Triangular panels can be used to add width at the Hip but not the Bust, or the opposite. They can be only a few inches [centimeters] long, adding critical inches only near the top or bottom of a side seam, or they can taper gradually over the full length of the seam.
- Diamond-shaped panels are useful if more width is needed at the waist than above or below.

To decide what sort of side panel you need, take a look at your sweater pattern. What are the finished measurements at the Bust, Waist, and Hip? Simply calculate your desired sweater measurements: your own Bust, Waist, and Hip measurements plus the desired amount of ease. The difference between the sweater's finished measurements and what you want them to be defines the size and shape of the side panel!

A Helpful Example

Time for a pretend Big Girl knitter to illustrate the B3 rules. Last year, our pretend Big Girl knit herself an intricately cabled sweater: a rectangular thing of beauty! (She didn't know better back then.) In the excitement of starting a new pattern, she completely forgot to check the dimensions of the finished sweater. In fact, she didn't check the finished measurements for the size she'd knitted until the pieces were done and something seemed not quite right. She'd thought an XL would fit her. That's the size she wears in all the clothing she buys at retail stores! But XL in this pattern was 6" [12.5cm] too narrow to fit her the way she wanted it to. Bugger.

The knitted pieces have been languishing in a pile of unfinished objects (UFOs). "What's the point of finishing the sweater?" she thinks. But wait, there's hope! Let's teach her how to knit some stockinette side panels.

First she needs some numbers. Sweaters that fit our knitter have a circumference of about 50" [127cm] at the Bust and Hips. Her actual Bust and Hips measure 46" [117cm]. Her beautifully knit but too-small sweater pieces are 22" [56cm] wide, yielding a sweater with a circumference of 44" [112cm].

Step 1: She figures out how much fabric she needs to add with her side panels.

- DSW (Desired Sweater Width) – ASW (Actual Sweater Width) = SWS (Sweater Width Shortfall)
- 50" [127cm] – 44" [112cm] = 6" [15cm]

So her side panels will total 6" [15cm] in width, 3" [7.5cm] wide each at their widest point. What does that translate to in stitches?

- 3" [7.5cm] panel x 4 stitches/1" [2.5cm] = 12 stitches + 2 selvedge stitches = 14 stitches

So, her side panels will be 14 stitches wide at the top and bottom. What are the 2 selvedge stitches for? One stitch is needed on each side of the panel so she can sew the panel into the side seam, leaving the full 3" [7.5cm] of each panel to do its job.

Our pretend Big Girl has an hourglass figure (but we like her anyway), which looks great with some waist shaping, so she'll make her side panels hourglass shaped as well. She shouldn't taper the panels down to nothing at the waist because then she wouldn't have enough fabric to sew the sweater together. Let's give her side panel a little less ease in the Waist portion than at the Bust and Hips. That way, it'll show off her hourglass figure even more! We'll taper each panel down to 1" [2.5cm] at the Waist.

- 1" (width of panel at Waist) x 4 stitches/inch [2.5cm] = 4 stitches + 2 selvedge stitches = 6 stitches

The panel is 14 stitches wide at the top and has to decrease to 6 stitches at the Waist. That's 8 stitches to decrease, then increase again. Because decreases have to be made on both sides of the panel, 8 total stitches/2 edges = 4 stitches to decrease from each edge. That's 4 decrease rows.

Step 2: How many rows does she decrease over?

- (LL [Lower Length, from Hem to Waist] – 1) x R = number of rows over which to work her decreases
- (6 – 1) x 6 = 30

So she has 30 rows to spread her decreases over. One Big Girl rule is to set aside 2" [5cm] at the Waist—1" [2.5cm] each from the LL and the UL (Upper Length, from Waist to Armhole)—to work the slimmest part of the piece, whether it's the front of a sweater with waist shaping or the hourglass-shaped side panel being worked here. She'll steal 2 rows from the 2" [5cm] she'd work at the "waist" of the side panel and add them to the lower section, so she has 32 rows to work her decreases over, just to make the math easier.

- 32 rows ÷ 4 decrease rows = 1 decrease row every 8 rows

See? That's a nice round number. Now she's got to increase back again. It goes like this:

- (UL – 1) x R = number of rows over which to work her increases
- (8 – 1) x 6 = 42

So she has 42 rows to spread her increases over. She can take 2 rows from this 42 and give them back to the 2" [5cm] of stockinette at the waist, which leaves her with 40 rows. This also makes her math tidier.

- 40 rows ÷ 4 increase rows = 1 increase row every 10 rows

Using all this information, here's how she would work this panel:

- **Cast on 14 stitches.** Work 1 row in stockinette. (This extra row is worked so the 1st row and decrease row can both be on the right side of the piece. We'll subtract this row from the rows at the waist section later.) Work 7 rows more in pattern.
- **Work a decrease row**: K1, k2tog, knit to last 3 stitches, ssk, k1. Repeat these 8 rows 3 times more; all 4 decrease rows have been worked. Now work 11 rows in stockinette stitch. This is the 2" [5cm] at the waist, less the 1 row added to the bottom of the piece.

- **Work an increase row:** K1, M1 (any increase will work), knit to last stitch, M1, k1. Work 9 rows in stockinette stitch. Repeat these 10 rows 3 times more; all 4 increase rows have been worked, and the side panel is finished!

"But," you ask, "what if she wants to knit a diamond-shaped or triangular panel instead of an hourglass-shaped one?" Good question! She would fill out her measurements in exactly the same way, no matter which shape she wanted. In fact, filling out her measurements would help her figure out which type of panel would serve her best. If she decided to work a diamond-shaped panel, she would work increase rows to reach the desired panel width at the Waist and decrease rows to obtain the right width at the underarm. If a triangular panel was in order, she would taper the panel down from the desired width at the hem to 2 stitches (for the seam allowances) at the Bust. Or, if she was making an inverted triangle, she would increase from 2 stitches at the hem to the desired number of stitches at the Bust. It's that easy.

Of course, changing the width of a sweater under the arm means the sleeve needs to be widened at the underarm as well, or it won't fit into the armhole. Our Big Girl needs to make a triangular sleeve panel to fit into the sleeve seam to widen it. How much does it need to be widened? It needs to start out as wide as the side panel at the underarm, so our Big Girl casts on 14 stitches. The panel needs to narrow gradually until only the 2 selvedge stitches remain. Having 12 stitches to decrease means she needs 6 decrease rows to decrease away all 12 stitches.

The sleeve panel itself should be at least one-third to one-half of the sleeve length. Her sleeve is 18" [15.5cm] long, so she wants the panel to be between 6" [15cm] and 9" [23cm] long. She decreases every 8 rows:

- 6 decrease rows worked every 8 rows = 48 rows
- 48 rows ÷ 6 rows/1" [2.5cm] = 8 inches [20.5cm].

Perfect length! After her side panels and sleeve panels are sewn into the side and sleeve seams, the sleeves will fit nicely into the armholes.

Our girl has now turned a beautifully textured, too-small rectangle into a curvy, cabled, beautifully textured sweater that fits her perfectly! Now it's your turn. Here's your chart!

MEASUREMENT	ABBREVIATION	EXAMPLE
BODY MEASUREMENT		
BUST	B	46"[117cm]
WAIST	W	42"[106.5cm]
HIPS	H	46"[117cm]
SWEATER MEASUREMENT		
STITCHES PER INCH [2.5cm]	S	4
ROWS PER INCH [2.5cm]	R	6
LOWER LENGTH (HEM TO WAIST)	LL	6"[15cm]
UPPER LENGTH (WAIST TO ARMHOLE)	UL	8"[20.5cm]
ACTUAL SWEATER WIDTH	ASW	44"[112cm]
DESIRED SWEATER WIDTH	DSW	50"[127cm]
SW SHORTFALL: DSW – ASW	SWS	6"[15cm]
SHORTFALL PER SIDE: SWS – 2	SPW	3"[15cm]
CONVERT SPW TO STITCHES: SPW x S + 2		14
DESIRED SPW AT WAIST	SPWw	1"[2.5cm]
CONVERT SPWw TO STITCHES: SPWw x S + 2		6

chapter two

PULLOVERS

This chapter is all about sweaters that shape and drape beautifully. For a sweater with a closer fit, try Annie Modesitt's Dark Victory Sweater in a soft merino wool. If you'd like something a little looser—but with flattering, figure-enhancing details— Lily Chin's Hourglass Pullover fits the bill. Throughout, you'll find subtle details— such as ruffles, cables, and cords—that draw the eye to your best features.

MARBLED TOP

by Berta Karapetyan

Knock pleats flat on their backs with this feathered turtleneck, which features rows of horizontal pleats—but only on the front. Pleats aligned around the armholes and the upper yoke enhance the top of your hourglass shape, and side shaping narrows your silhouette toward the waist. Pick a comfy yarn and make this top a classic in your wardrobe!

Skill Level
Experienced

Sizes
S (M, L, XL)

Finished Measurements
Bust: 33 (36, 39, 42)" [84 (91, 99, 106)cm]
Length: 23½, (24, 24½, 25)" [60 (61, 62, 63.5) cm]
Upper arm: 11 (12, 13, 14)" [28 (30.5, 33, 35.5) cm]

Materials
760 (855, 855, 950) yd [696 (783, 783, 870)m]
8 (9, 9, 10) balls Karabella Marble (55% wool, 45% superfine alpaca, each approximately 1¾ oz [50g] and 95 yd [87m]), in color #35353 Pink, **(4)** medium/worsted weight
1 Size 9 [5.5mm] circular needle, 24" [60cm] long, or size needed to obtain gauge
1 Size 1 [2.25mm] circular needle, 24" [60cm] long, or any small circular needle to be used as a stitch-holding needle
1 Size 8 [5mm] circular needle, 16" [40cm] long
Stitch holders
Yarn needle

Gauge
18 stitches and 22 rows = 4" [10cm] over stockinette stitch using size 9 [5.5mm] circular needle

Pattern Note
Although the body pieces are worked flat, circular needles are used to make it easier to align and work both sets of stitches when making the horizontal pleats.

Pattern Stitch
Horizontal Pleat
Rows 1 and 5 (RS): Knit.
Rows 2, 4, and 6: Purl.
Row 3 (eyelet row): K1, *k2tog, yo; repeat from * to last st, k1.
Using a stitch-holding needle and WS facing, pick up the same number of stitches as on main needle from 3rd row below eyelet row just knitted (i.e., the cast-on edge of the beginning hem and 3 rows below the eyelet row when making Horizontal Pleats).
Row 7: With both needles held parallel in your nondominant hand, knit together 1 st from the main needle with 1 st from the holding needle.

Instructions

Back
With the size 9 needle, cast on 70 (78, 86, 94) stitches.
Rows 1 and 5 (RS): Knit.
Rows 2, 4, and 6: Purl.
Row 3 (eyelet row): K1, *k2tog, yo; repeat from * to last stitch, k1.
With the stitch-holding needle and WS facing, pick up 70 (78, 86, 94) stitches from cast-on edge.

Row 7 (RS): With both needles held parallel in your nondominant hand, knit together 1 stitch from the main needle with 1 stitch from the stitch-holding needle.
Work even in stockinette stitch for 9 rows.
Decrease row (RS): K2, k2tog, knit to last 4 stitches, ssk, k2—68 (76, 84, 92) stitches.
Repeat this decrease row every 10 rows twice more—64 (72, 80, 88) stitches.
Work even in stockinette stitch for 9 rows.

Increase row (RS): K2, M1, knit to last 2 stitches, M1, k2—66 (74, 82, 90) stitches.
Repeat this increase row every 10 rows 3 times more—72 (80, 88, 96) stitches.
Work even until piece measures 15" [38cm] from cast-on edge, ending after working a WS row.

Shape Armholes

Next 2 rows: Bind off 4 (4, 5, 5) stitches, work to end—64 (72, 78, 86) stitches.
Decrease row (RS): K2, k2tog, knit to last 4 stitches, ssk, k2—62 (70, 76, 84) stitches.
Repeat this decrease row every other row 2 (3, 3, 4) times more—58 (64, 70, 76) stitches.
Work even until armhole measures 7½ (8, 8½, 9)" [19 (20.5, 21.5, 23)cm].

Shape Shoulders

Next 2 rows: Bind off 6 (6, 7, 8) stitches, work in pattern as established—46 (52, 56, 60) stitches.
Next 2 rows: Bind off 5 (6, 7, 7) stitches, work in pattern as established—36 (40, 42, 46) stitches.
Next 2 rows: Bind off 5 (6, 6, 7) stitches, work in pattern as established.
Place remaining 26 (28, 30, 32) stitches on a stitch holder for Back Neck.

Front

Work as for Back until armhole decreases are completed and there are 58 (64, 70, 76) stitches on the needle, ending after working a WS row.
Next 7 rows: Work 1 Horizontal Pleat (centering the eyelet row by picking up stitches 3 rows below the eyelet row).
Work even in stockinette stitch for 11 rows more, ending after working a WS row.
Next 7 rows: Work 1 Horizontal Pleat.
Work even until armhole measures 5 (5½, 6, 6½)" [12.5 (14, 15, 16.5)cm], ending after working a WS row.

Shape Neck and Shoulders

Decrease row (RS): K18 (20, 22, 24), k2tog, k1, place next 16 (18, 20, 22) stitches on stitch holder, join 2nd ball of yarn, k1, ssk, k18 (20, 22, 24)—20 (22, 24, 26) stitches on each side of neck.

Working both sides at once, repeat this decrease row every other row 4 times more—16 (18, 20, 22) stitches each side of neck.

Work even until armhole measures 7½ (8, 8½, 9)" [19 (20.5, 21.5, 23)cm], ending after working a WS row. Shape Shoulders as for Back.

Sleeve (Make 2)

Cast on 40 (42, 44, 46) stitches.

Rows 1 and 5 (RS): Knit.

Rows 2, 4, and 6: Purl.

Row 3 (eyelet row): K1, *k2tog, yo; repeat from * to last stitch, k1.

With stitch-holding needle and WS facing, pick up 40 (42, 44, 46) stitches from cast-on row.

Row 7 (RS): With both needles held parallel in your nondominant hand, knit together 1 stitch from the main needle with 1 stitch from the stitch-holding needle.

Work in stockinette stitch for 17 rows more, ending after working a WS row.

Next 7 rows: Work Horizontal Pleat.

Work Horizontal Pleat every 17 rows twice more.

Work even in stockinette stitch for 7 rows more.

Increase row (RS): K2, M1, knit to last 2 stitches, M1, k2—42 (44, 45, 48) stitches.

Repeat this increase row every 8 (6, 6, 4) rows 4 (5, 6, 7) times more—50 (54, 58, 62) stitches.

Work even until piece measures 19" [48cm], ending after working a WS row.

Shape Cap

Next 2 rows: Bind off 4 (4, 5, 5) stitches, work in pattern as established—40 (46, 48, 52) stitches.

Decrease row (RS): K2, ssk, knit to last 4 stitches, k2tog, k2—38 (44, 46, 50) stitches.

Repeat this decrease row every other row until 10 stitches remain.

Bind off remaining stitches.

Finishing

Using a yarn needle, sew shoulder seams.

Turtleneck

With RS facing and size 8 [5mm] circular needle, work across 26 (28, 30, 32) stitches from back neck holder, pick up 10 stitches along right side edge of neck, work across 16 (18, 20, 22) stitches from front neck holder, pick up 10 stitches from left side edge of neck 62 (66, 70, 74) stitches.

Join stitches in the round, and work in circular stockinette stitch (knit every round) for 4" [10cm].

Next round (eyelet round): *K2tog, yo; repeat from * to end of round.

Work 3 rounds more in stockinette stitch.

Bind off loosely.

Fold the turtleneck edge to WS at eyelet round and sew in place, carefully matching knitting tension.

Sew Sleeves into armholes.

Sew side and Sleeve seams.

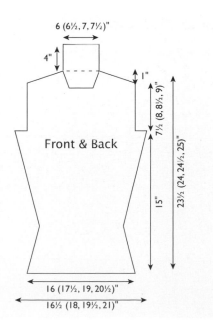

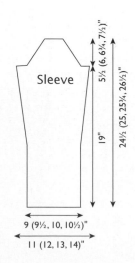

ROMAN CANDLE PULLOVER

by Berta Karapetyan

This basket-weave sweater has a wonderful texture that stands out against the red of the yarn. The 2x2 ribbing pattern hugs the lower body and lower sleeve so you'll be ready when this supersoft turtleneck attracts the attention of its firework namesake!

Skill Level
Experienced

Sizes
S (M, L, XL)

Finished Measurements
Bust: 33 (36, 39, 42)" [84 (91.5, 99, 106.5)cm]
Length: 22 (22½, 23, 23½)" [56 (57, 58.5, 59.5)cm]
Upper arm: 11 (12, 13, 14)" [28 (30.5, 33, 35.5)cm]

Materials
978 (1141, 1141, 1304) yd [900 (1050, 1050, 1200)m] / 6 (7, 7, 8) balls Karabella Boise (50% cashmere, 50% merino wool, each approximately 1¾ oz [50g] and 163 yd [150m]), in color #63 Burgundy, (**3**) light/DK weight
1 Pair size 3 [3.25mm] needles
1 Pair size 8 [5mm] needles, or size needed to obtain gauge
1 Size 4 [3.5mm] circular needle, 16" [40cm] long
Cable needle
Stitch holders
Stitch markers
Yarn needle

Gauge
32 stitches and 24 rows = 4" [10cm] over Basket Pattern 1 using larger needles

Pattern Stitches
2x2 Rib (over a multiple of 4 stitches + 2)
Row 1 (RS): K1, *p2, k2; repeat from * to end.
Row 2 (WS): P2, *k2, p2; repeat from * to end.
Repeat Rows 1 and 2 for 2x2 Rib.

Basket Pattern 1 (over a multiple of 6 stitches + 5)
Row 1 (RS): K4, *slip 3 stitches onto cable needle and hold to front, k3, k3 from cable needle; repeat from * to last stitch, k1.
Row 2 and all WS rows: Purl.
Rows 3 and 7: Knit.
Row 5: K1, *slip 3 stitches onto cable needle and hold to back, k3, k3 from cable needle; repeat from * to last 4 stitches, k4.
Row 8: Purl.
Repeat Rows 1–8 for Basket Pattern 1.

Basket Pattern 2 (over a multiple of 6 stitches + 5)
Row 1 (RS): K1, *slip 3 stitches onto cable needle and hold to front, k3, k3 from cable needle; repeat from * to last 4 stitches, k4.
Row 2 and all WS rows: Purl.
Rows 3 and 7: Knit.
Row 5: K4, *slip 3 stitches onto cable needle and hold to back, k3, k3 from cable needle; repeat from * to last stitch, k1.
Row 8: Purl.
Repeat Rows 1–8 for Basket Pattern 2.

Instructions

Back

With size 3 straight needles, cast on 102 (114, 126, 138) stitches and work in 2x2 Rib for 6" [15cm], ending after working a WS row.
Change to size 8 straight needles and increase 29 stitches evenly spaced as follows:

Size S only
Increase row (RS): K3, M1, *k3, M1, k4, M1; repeat from * to last stitch, k1—131 stitches.

Size M Only
Increase row (RS): K1, M1, *k4, M1; repeat from * to last stitch, k1—143 stitches.

Size L Only

Increase row (RS): (K5, M1) twice, *k4, M1; repeat from * to last 16 stitches, k5, M1, k6, M1, k5—155 stitches.

Size XL Only

Increase row (RS): K6, M1, *k5, M1, k4, M1; repeat from * to last 6 stitches, k6—167 stitches.

For All Sizes

Purl next row.
Work in Basket Pattern 1 for approximately 7½" [19cm], ending after working Row 4 (WS) of Basket Pattern 1.

Shape Armholes

Next 2 rows: Bind off 6 stitches, work in pattern as established—119 (131, 143, 155) stitches.
Next 4 rows: Bind off 3 stitches, work in pattern as established—107 (119, 131, 143) stitches.
Work even in Basket Pattern 1 until armhole measures approximately 7½ (8, 8½, 9)" [19 (20.5, 31.5, 23)cm] from 1st bind-off row, ending after working Row 4 (WS) of Basket Pattern 1.

Shape Shoulders

Next 4 rows: Bind off 11 (13, 14, 16), work in pattern as established—63 (67, 75, 79) stitches.
Next 2 rows: Bind off 10 (12, 13, 15), work in pattern as established—43 (43, 49, 49) stitches.
Place remaining 43 (43, 49, 49) stitches on a stitch holder for back neck.

Front

Work as for Back until armhole measures approximately 6½ (7, 7½, 8)" [16.5 (18, 19, 20.5) cm], ending after working pattern Row 4 (WS) of Basket Pattern 1—107 (119, 131, 143) stitches.

Shape Neck

Row 1 (RS): K1, work Row 5 of Basket Pattern 1 from * to * for 36 (42, 48, 54) stitches, k4 (4, 1, 1), place next 25 (25, 31, 31) stitches on a stitch holder for front neck; join 2nd ball of yarn and k1 (1, 4, 4), work Row 5 of Basket Pattern 1 from * to * for 36 (42, 48, 54) stitches, to last stitch, k1.
Work both sides at the same time as follows:
Rows 2, 4, and 6: Purl to neck edge for opposite side of neck, bind off 3 stitches, purl to end.
Row 3: Knit to neck edge; for opposite side of neck, bind off 3 stitches, knit to end.

Row 5: K4, work Row 1 of pattern from * to * to last 1 (1, 4, 4) stitches, k1 (1, 4, 4); for opposite side of neck, bind off 3 stitches, k4 (1, 4, 1) stitches, work Row 1 of pattern from * to * to last 1 stitch, k1.
Row 7: Work Row 3.

Shape Shoulders

Work as for Back.

Sleeve (Make 2)

With size 3 straight needles, cast on 62 (66, 70, 74) stitches. Work in 2x2 Rib for 8" [20.5cm], ending after working a WS row. Change to size 8 straight needles and increase 21 (23, 25, 27) stitches evenly spaced as follows:

Size S Only

Increase row (RS): (K2, M1, k3, M1) 4 times, (k5, M1) 3 times, (k2, M1, k3, M1) 5 times, k2—83 stitches.

Size M Only

Increase row (RS): (K3, M1, k2, M1) 5 times, (k5, M1) twice, (k3, M1, k2, M1) 5 times, k3, M1, k3—89 stitches.

Size L Only

Increase row (RS): (K3, M1, k2, M1) 5 times, (k5, M1) twice, (k3, M1, k2, M1) 6 times, k3, M1, k2—95 stitches.

Size XL Only

Increase row (RS): (K3, M1, k2, M1) 6 times, (k5, M1) twice, (k3, M1, k2, M1) 6 times, k3, M1, k1—101 stitches.

For All Sizes

Purl next row.
Begin Basket Pattern 1 and work 14 rows, ending on a WS row.
Increase row (RS): K1, M1, place marker, knit to last stitch, place marker, M1, k1—85 (91, 97, 103) stitches.
Repeat this increase row every 16th row (Row 7 of Basket Pattern 1) twice more, ending on a WS row and dropping markers on the last row—89 (95, 101, 107) stitches.
Work even in Basket Pattern 2, beginning with Row 1, until piece measures approximately 18"

[46cm] from cast-on edge, ending after working Row 8 of Basket Pattern 2 (WS).

Shape Cap

Next 2 rows: Bind off 6 stitches, work in pattern as established—77 (83, 89, 95) stitches.

Next 4 rows: Bind off 3 stitches, work in pattern as established—65 (71, 77, 83) stitches.

Work in pattern as established until cap measures approximately 4½ (5, 5½, 6)" [11 (12.5, 14, 15) cm], ending after working a WS row.

Bind off 3 stitches at the beginning of the next 8 rows, then work the remaining stitches in pattern—41 (47, 53, 59) stitches.

Bind off the remaining stitches.

Finishing

Using a yarn needle, sew shoulder seams.

Turtleneck

With RS facing and circular needle, k43 (43, 49, 49) stitches from back neck holder, pick up and knit 16 stitches along left neck edge, k25 (25, 31, 31) stitches from front neck holder, pick up and knit 16 stitches along right neck edge—100 (100, 112, 112) stitches.

Join in round and work in 2x2 Rib for 5" [12.5cm].

Bind off tightly.

Sew in Sleeves into armholes.

Sew side and Sleeve seams.

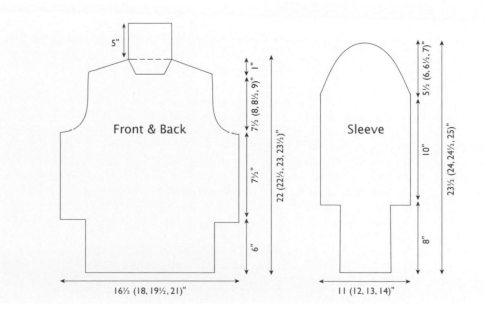

DARK VICTORY SWEATER

by Annie Modesitt

When a wool is as soft, luxurious, and stunningly dyed as this, it begs to be worn close to the body! Shaping at the bust, hips, and waist emphasize a womanly form, and neckline colorwork details draw attention to the face and throat.

Skill Level
Intermediate

Sizes
XS (S, M, L, 1X, 2X)

Finished Measurements
Bust: 33 (37, 41, 45, 51, 57)" [84 (94, 104, 114.5, 129.5, 145)cm]
Length: 24½ (25, 26¼, 27¾, 29½, 30¼)" [62 (63.5, 66.5, 70.5, 75, 77)cm]

Materials
Malabrigo Merino Worsted (100% pure Merino wool, each approximately 3½ oz [100g] and 216 yd [197m]), (4) medium/worsted weight 851 (918, 996, 1078, 1192, 1292) yd [776 (837, 909, 983, 1087, 1179)m] / 4 (5, 5, 6, 6, 7) balls in color #41 Burgundy (A)
106 (115, 125, 135, 149, 162) yd [97 (105, 114, 123, 136, 148)m] / 1 (1, 1, 1, 1, 1) ball in color #35 Frank Ochre (B)
106 (115, 125, 135, 149, 162) yd [97 (105, 114, 123, 136, 148)m)] / 1 (1, 1, 1, 1, 1) ball in color #53 Peach Tree (C)
1 Size 7 [4.5mm] circular needle, 36" [91cm] long
1 Size 8 [5mm] circular needle, 36" [91cm] long, or size needed to obtain gauge

Stitch markers in yellow and blue
Stitch holders
Yarn needle
36" [91.5cm] length of ribbon to thread through yoke (optional)

Gauge
17 stitches and 24 rows = 4" [10cm] over stockinette stitch using larger circular needle

Stitch Glossary
Twisted Float Right Slant: Working on the WS and keeping yarn to the RS of the work, knit 1 with A, drop strand, *bring a strand of B *over* a hanging strand of A, knit 1 with B, bring a strand of A *over* strand of B, knit 1 with A; repeat from * to last stitch, knit 1 with B.
Twisted Float Left Slant: Working on the WS and keeping yarn to the RS of the work, knit 1 with A, drop strand, *bring strand of B *under* hanging strand of A, knit 1 with B, bring strand of A *under* strand of B, knit 1 with A; repeat from * to last stitch, knit 1 with B.
Note: Working a round of Twisted Float Left Slant will untwist the strands that have spiraled around each other in the Twisted Float Right Slant round.

Instructions

Body
With smaller needle and A, cast on 144 (160, 176, 192, 216, 240) stitches. Join stitches, placing marker to indicate the beginning of the round. Work in a 2x2 Rib (page **134**) for 2 rounds, increasing 2 stitches evenly spaced around last round—146 (162, 178, 194, 218, 242) stitches. Change to larger needle.

Establish Slip-Stitch Colorwork Pattern (Chart A)
Establish ribbing pattern (RS): With A, k1, *p2, k2, repeat from * over next 36 (40, 44, 48, 56, 60) stitches, k1, place yellow marker, k35 (39, 43, 47, 51, 59) stitches, place yellow marker, k1, (p2, k2) over next 36 (40, 44, 48, 56, 60) stitches,

k1, place blue marker, k35 (39, 43, 47, 51, 59) stitches to end of round.
Rounds 1 and 3: With A, work in ribbing pattern to yellow marker, slip marker, k1, *slip 1, p1; repeat from * to 1 stitch before next yellow marker, k1, slip marker, work in ribbing pattern to next marker, slip marker, k1, *slip 1, p1; repeat from * to 1 stitch before end of round, k1.
Rounds 2 and 4: With B, work in ribbing pattern as established and stockinette stitch between the yellow markers over slip-stitch sections.
Repeat last 4 rounds until piece measures 3¾ (3¾, 4, 4, 4¼, 4½)" [9.5 (9.5, 10, 10, 11, 11.5)cm] from cast-on edge.
Note: The yellow markers indicate the edges of the center front panel; the decreases for hip shaping

and increases for bust shaping happen on either side of the yellow markers. The blue markers denote the edges of the center back panel; the decrease for hip shaping happens on either side of the blue markers.

Shape Sides

Next round: With A only, work in patterns as established (ribbing pattern to marker, slip marker, ssk, in pattern to 2 stitches before next marker, k2tog, slip marker) twice—140 (156, 172, 188, 212, 236) stitches (4 stitches decreased).

Next 3 rounds: Work even (no shaping) in pattern as established, always working stitches on either side of markers as knit stitches.

Repeat last 4 rounds until 124 (140, 156, 176, 200, 224) stitches remain.

Work even until piece measures 11¾ (11¾, 12½, 13, 13¾, 14)" [30 (30, 32, 33, 35, 35.5)cm] from cast-on edge.

Next round: Work in ribbing pattern as established to yellow marker, slip marker, increase 1 stitch, work in pattern to next yellow marker, increase 1 stitch, slip marker, work remaining stitches in patterns as established—126 (142, 158, 178, 202, 226) stitches (2 stitches increased).

Next round: Work in pattern as established, always working stitches on either side of marker as knit stitches.

Repeat last 2 rounds until 144 (160, 176, 192, 216, 240) stitches remain.

AT THE SAME TIME, when piece measures 19¾ (19¾, 21, 22, 23¼, 23½)" [50 (50, 53.5, 56, 59, 59.5)cm] from cast-on edge, divide Front and Back as follows.

Next round: *Work 15 (17, 19, 21, 23, 27) stitches in ribbing pattern as established, bind off 6 stitches, work 15 (17, 19, 21, 23, 27) stitches to next marker, work in pattern as established to next marker; repeat from * once more.

Slip the remaining 60 (68, 76, 84, 96, 108) stitches at Front and Back to stitch holders.

Sleeve (Make 2)

With smaller needle and A, cast on 34 (34, 34, 38, 38, 42) stitches. Work back and forth as follows:

Row 1 (RS): K1, (p2, k2); repeat to last stitch, k1.

Change to larger needle and work in ribbing pattern as established, k4, increase 1 stitch, place marker, work to last 4 stitches, place marker, increase 1 stitch, work to end of row.

Next row (WS): Work in ribbing pattern as established.

Next row (RS): Work to marker, increase 1 stitch, slip marker, work to next marker in ribbing pattern as established, slip marker, increase 1 stitch, work to end of row.

Continue in this manner, increasing 1 stitch at each edge every 4 rows a total of 22 (23, 24, 24, 26, 25) times, incorporating new stitches into ribbing pattern—78 (80, 82, 86, 90, 92) stitches. Work even until piece measures 16¼ (16½, 16¾, 17, 17½, 18)" [41 (42, 42.5, 43, 44.5, 45.5)cm] from cast-on edge.

Next 2 rows: Bind off 6 stitches, work in pattern as established—66 (68, 70, 74, 78, 80) stitches.

Yoke
Joining Round

Slip all pieces onto 1 needle: 60 (68, 76, 84, 96, 108) stitches of Front, 66 (68, 70, 74, 78, 80) stitches of one Sleeve, 60 (68, 76, 84, 96, 108) stitches of Back, 66 (68, 70, 74, 78, 80) stitches of other Sleeve—252 (272, 292, 316, 348, 376) stitches.

Set-up round: With A, knit, increasing 4 (0, 4, 4, 4, 0) stitches evenly around work—256 (272, 296, 320, 352, 376) stitches.

Round 1: Knit, placing a marker every 32 (34, 37, 40, 44, 47) stitches and a contrasting marker to indicate beginning of round—8 markers total.

Round 2: Purl all stitches, decreasing 1 stitch between each set of markers—248 (264, 288, 312, 344, 368) stitches.

Round 3: With C, knit.

Round 4: Purl.

Repeat Rounds 1–4—240 (256, 280, 304, 360) stitches.

Begin Twisted Float Band (Chart B)

Round 1 (WS): Turn work so WS is facing. With A and B, work Twisted Float Right Slant around all stitches. (**Note:** Yarn strands will twist.)

Round 2 (WS): Continuing on the WS, work Twisted Float Left Slant. (**Note:** Yarn strands will untwist.)

Repeat Rounds 1 and 2 once.

With A and C, repeat Rounds 1 and 2 twice more (8 rounds total), then turn piece so that RS is facing you. Change to smaller needles and A.

Knit 1 round.

Purl 1 round.

Next round: *K4, p4; repeat from * around.

Work a k4, p4 ribbing pattern for 3 rounds.

Next round: *K4, p1, p2tog, p1; repeat from * around—210 (224, 245, 266, 294, 315) stitches.

Work in a k4, p3 ribbing pattern for 3 rounds.

Next round: *K1, k2tog, k1, p3; repeat from * around—180 (192, 210, 228, 252, 270) stitches.

Work in a k3, p3 ribbing pattern for 3 rounds.

Next round: *K4, p2tog, p1; repeat from * around—150 (160, 175, 190, 210, 225) stitches.

Work in a k3, p2 ribbing pattern for 3 rounds.

Next round: *K2tog, k1, p3; repeat from * around—120 (128, 140, 152, 168, 180) stitches.

Work in 2x2 Rib for 3 rounds.

Change to smaller needles. With C, work in ribbing pattern as established until Yoke measures 4¾ (5¼, 5¼, 5¾, 6¼, 6¾)" [12 (13.5, 13.5, 14.5, 16, 17)cm] from joining round. Bind off all stitches loosely in ribbing pattern.

Finishing

Using a yarn needle, sew underarm seams.

Steam-block piece to measurements.

Thread ribbon (or several strands of yarn) through yarn overs at Yoke, if desired.

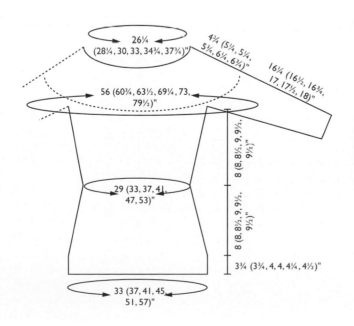

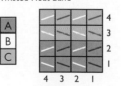

Chart A
Slip–Stitch Colorwork Pattern Repeat

Chart B
Twisted Float Band

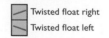

Twisted float right

Twisted float left

Purl 1

Knit 1

Slip stitch

CECILIA'S SWEATER

by Melissa Matthay

Trendy and casual, this sweater features cables used in a totally flattering manner: running vertically on both the front and the back. Of course, you can add or remove cables as you see fit. Shaping along the side edge of the body adds definition to the waistline.

Skill Level
Experienced

Sizes
S (M, L, XL)

Finished Measurements
Bust: 36 (39, 43, 47)" [91.5 (99, 109, 119)cm]
Length: 20½ (22, 22½, 24)" [52 (56, 57, 61)cm]
Upper arm: 14 (15½, 16, 16½)" [35.3 (39.5, 40.5, 42)cm]

Materials
781 (852, 923, 1065) yd / [704 (768, 832, 960) m] / 11 (12, 13, 15) skeins Tahki/Stacy Charles Collection Victoria (60% cotton, 40% viscose, each approximately 1¾ oz [50g] and 71 yd [64m]), in color #1 Bleach, (**4**) medium/worsted weight

1 Pair size 7 [4.5mm] needles
1 Pair size 9 [5.5mm] needles, or size needed to obtain gauge
Cable needle
Yarn needle

Gauge
17 stitches and 21 rows = 4" [10cm] over stockinette stitch using larger needles

Pattern Note
For smooth seams, work increases 2 stitches in from the edge of each row.

Stitch Glossary
C4: Slip 2 stitches onto cable needle and hold to the back of the work, k2, k2 from cable needle.

Instructions

Back

With smaller needles, cast on 76 (84, 92, 100) stitches.
Work in 1×1 Rib (page **134**) for 1" [2.5cm]. Change to larger needles.
Row 1 (RS): With larger needles, knit across the row.
Row 2: Purl
Row 3: *K16 (18, 20, 22), C4; repeat from * twice more, k16 (18, 20, 22).
Row 4: Purl.
Repeat Rows 1–4 for pattern.
AT THE SAME TIME, decrease 1 stitch at each edge every 8th row 3 times—70 (78, 86, 94) stitches.
Work even until piece measures 8 (9, 10, 11)" [20.5 (23, 25.5, 28)cm] from cast-on edge, ending after working a WS row.
Increase 1 stitch at each edge every 8th row 3 times—76 (84, 92, 100) stitches.
Work even until piece measures 13 (14, 14, 15)" [33 (35.5, 35.5, 38)cm] from cast-on edge, ending after working a WS row.

Shape Armholes

Next 2 rows: Bind off 4 stitches, work in pattern as established to the end of the row—68 (76, 84, 92) stitches.
Decrease 1 stitch at each edge every other row 4 (5, 5, 6) times—60 (66, 76, 80) stitches.
AT THE SAME TIME, work the cable every 4th row, moving side cables 1 stitch toward the center cable. (Knit 1 stitch more before the 1st cable, 1 stitch less between the 1st and center cables, 1 stitch less between the center and 3rd cables, and 1 stitch more after the 3rd cable than in the previous cable row.)
Work in pattern as established until piece measures 20½ (22, 22½, 24)" [52 (56, 57, 61)cm] from cast-on edge, ending after working a WS row.

Shape Shoulders

Next 2 rows: Bind off 12 (14, 16, 18) stitches, work in pattern as established to the end of the row—36 (38, 44, 44) stitches.
Work even in pattern for 1" [2.5cm]. Bind off very loosely.

Front

Work as for the Back.

Sleeve (Make 2)

With smaller needles, cast on 36 (38, 40, 42) stitches. Work in 1x1 Rib for 1" [2.5cm]. Change to larger needles. Work in pattern as follows:

Row 1: (RS): Knit.

Row 2: Purl.

Row 3: K16 (17, 18, 19), C4, k16 (17 18, 19).

Row 4: Purl.

Repeat Rows 1-4 for pattern.

AT THE SAME TIME, increase 1 stitch at each edge every 6th row 13 (13, 14, 15) times—62 (64, 68, 72) stitches.

Work even in pattern as established until piece measures 16 (16½, 16½, 17)" [40.5 (42, 42, 43) cm] from cast-on edge, ending after working a WS row.

Shape Cap

Next 2 rows: Bind off 4 stitches, work in pattern as established to the end of the row—54 (56, 60, 64) stitches.

Decrease 1 stitch at each edge every other row 13 (13, 14, 15) times—28 (30, 32, 34) stitches.

Next 4 rows: Bind off 2 stitches, work in pattern as established to the end of the row —20 (22, 24, 26) stitches.

Bind off all stitches.

Finishing

Using a yarn needle, sew shoulder seams.
Sew in Sleeves into armholes.
Sew side and Sleeve seams.

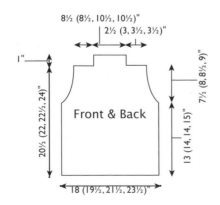

8½ (8½, 10½, 10½)"

2½ (3, 3½, 3½)"

1"

Front & Back

20½ (22, 22½, 24)"

7½ (8, 8½, 9)"

13 (14, 14, 15)"

18 (19½, 21½, 23½)"

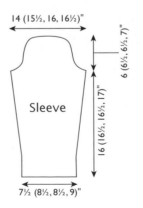

14 (15½, 16, 16½)"

6 (6½, 6½, 7)"

Sleeve

16 (16½, 16½, 17)"

7½ (8½, 8½, 9)"

HOURGLASS PULLOVER

by Lily Chin

The slimming lines of this shapely tunic create the illusion traditional princess seaming without having to sew. Add the collar to draw attention upward toward the face.

Skill Level
Experienced

Sizes
S (M, L, 1X, 2X)

Finished Measurements
Bust: 35 (38, 41, 44, 47)" [89 (96.5, 104, 111.5, 119.5)cm]
Length: 21½ (22, 22½, 23, 23½)" [54.5 (56, 57, 58.5, 59.5)cm]
Sleeve length (including cap): 22½ (22, 21¾, 21½, 21½)" [57 (56, 55, 54.5, 54.5)cm]

Materials
1143 (1270, 1397, 1651, 1778) yd [1044 (1160, 1276, 1508, 1624)m] / 9 (10, 11, 13, 14) balls Lily Chin Signature Collection Gramercy (100% superwash merino wool, each approximately 1¾ oz [50g] and 127 yd [116m]), in color #3624 Cranberry, (3) light/DK weight
1 Pair size 5 [3.75mm] needles, or size needed to obtain gauge
1 Pair size 6 [4mm] needles, or size needed to obtain gauge
1 Size 5 [3.75mm] circular needle, 16" [41cm] long
Yarn needle
6 Buttons, 1" [25mm] wide

Gauge
22 stitches and 28 rows = 4" [10cm] over stockinette stitch using larger needles
22 stitches = 4" [10cm] over Seed Stitch using smaller needles

Pattern Note
Many things are happening at once (e.g., side shaping and center panel patterning). It is strongly suggested that you create a full stitch chart using several sheets of graph paper taped together to keep track of all the shaping and pattern instructions.

Pattern Stitch
Seed Stitch (over an odd number of stitches)
Row 1: K1, *p1, k1; repeat from * to end.
Row 2: Knit the purl stitches and purl the knit stitches.
Repeat Row 2 for Seed Stitch.

Stitch Glossary
M1p (make 1 purl stitch): Lift the horizontal bar between stitches and purl it through the back loop to increase 1 stitch.

Instructions

Back
Edging
With the smaller straight needles, cast on 99 (107, 115, 123, 131) stitches.
Work in Seed Stitch for 1" [2.5cm], ending after working a WS row.

Body
Change to larger needles.
Row 1 (RS): K2, p19 (23, 27, 31, 34), k57 (57, 57, 57, 59) for center panel, p19 (23, 27, 31, 34), k2.
Notes: In subsequent rows, maintain this pattern of stockinette stitch over stockinette and reverse stockinette stitch over reverse stockinette unless otherwise directed for center panel. Always keep 2 stitches in stockinette stitch at the end of each row.
Work 6 (6, 6, 8, 5) rows in pattern as established.

Create Center Panel Pattern
Next row: Change 1 stitch at each end of the center panel from stockinette to reverse stockinette—55 (55, 55, 55, 57) center panel stitches in stockinette.
Change 1 stitch at each end of center panel from stockinette to reverse stockinette every 5th row 6 (6, 6, 6, 7) times more—43 center panel stitches in stockinette.
Work 11 (11, 9, 9, 9) rows even.
Change 1 stitch at each end of center panel from reverse stockinette to stockinette—45 center panel stitches in stockinette.
Change 1 stitch at each end of center panel from reverse stockinette to stockinette [every 6th row, then every 7th row] 2 (2, 0, 0, 0) times more, every 6th row 1 (1, 0, 0, 0) time, every 5th row 7 (10, 18, 6, 0) times, then every 4th row 0 (0, 1, 14, 23) times.

AT THE SAME TIME, after 6 (6, 6, 8, 8) rows of Body have been completed, begin to shape waist as follows.

Shape Waist

Decrease 1 stitch at both ends of each row with fully fashioned decreases (made 1 stitch in from edge), as follows:

Next row (RS): K1, ssk, work in pattern to within last 3 stitches, k2tog, k1—97 (105, 113, 121, 129) stitches.

Work center panel pattern and decrease in this same manner every 8th row 0 (0, 0, 1, 2) time(s) more, then every 6th row 5 (5, 5, 4, 3) times. Work even on 87 (95, 103, 111, 119) stitches until piece measures 7¾ (7, 7¼, 7½, 8)" [19.5 (17.5, 18.5, 19, 20.5)cm] from cast-on edge, ending after working a WS row.

Increase 1 stitch at both ends of each row with fully fashioned increases (2 stitches in from edge) as follows:

K2, M1p, work in pattern to within last 2 stitches, M1p, k2—89 (97, 105, 113, 121) stitches.

Work center panel pattern, increasing 1 stitch at both ends of each row as established every 4th row 0, (0, 0, 0, 1) times, then every 6th row 5 (5, 5, 5, 4) times.

Work even in pattern on 99 (107, 115, 123, 131) stitches until piece measures 13" [33cm] from cast-on edge.

Shape Armholes

Next 2 rows: Bind off 5 (6, 6, 7, 7) stitches, work center panel pattern as established—89 (95, 103, 109, 117) stitches.

Work center panel pattern as established while AT THE SAME TIME binding off 3 stitches at the beginning of the next 0 (0, 0, 2, 2) rows, then 2 stitches at the beginning of the next 2 (0, 2, 2, 2) rows—85 (95, 99, 99, 107) stitches.

Decrease row: Work 1 fully fashioned decrease at the beginning and end of the next RS row. Repeat the decrease row every other row 5 (8, 6, 3, 4) times, then every 4th row 1 (0, 1, 2, 2) times—73 (79, 85, 89, 95) stitches. Work even in center panel pattern until armhole measures 7½ (8, 8½, 9, 9½)" [19 (20.5, 21.5, 23, 24)cm], ending ready to work a WS row.

Shape Shoulders and Neck

Next row (WS): Work even in pattern as established across 19 (22, 24, 26, 28) stitches, join a 2nd ball of yarn, bind off 35 (35, 37, 37, 39) stitches, work in pattern as established.

Bind off 2 stitches at the beginning of each row once, and decrease 1 stitch from each neck edge on the next RS row, then every other row once more.

AT THE SAME TIME, shape shoulders as follows:

Next 4 rows: Bind off 3 (3, 4, 5, 6) stitches, work in pattern as established.

Next 6 rows: Bind off 3 (4, 4, 4, 4) stitches, work in pattern as established.

Front

Work as for Back, including all shaping. AT THE SAME TIME, when piece measures 18½ (19, 19½, 20, 20½)" [47 (48, 49.5, 51, 52)cm] from cast-on edge, ending ready to work a WS row, shape neck as follows.

Shape Neck

Next row (RS): Work in pattern across 26 (29, 32, 34, 37) stitches, attach a 2nd ball of yarn, bind off center 21 stitches, work to end.

Working the center panel pattern on both sides of the neck at the same time, bind off 3 stitches from each neck edge once, then 2 stitches once. Work center panel pattern with 1 fully fashioned decrease at each neck edge on next RS row, then every other row 5 (5, 6, 6, 7) times more.

AT SAME TIME, when piece measures 20½ (21, 21½, 22, 22½)" [52 (53.5, 54.5, 56, 57)cm] from cast-on edge, ending ready to work a RS row—15 (18, 20, 22, 24) stitches each side.

Shape Shoulders

Work as for Back.

Sleeve (Make 2)

Edging

With smaller needles, cast on 47 (49, 51, 53, 55) stitches.

Work in Seed Stitch for 1" [2.5cm] from cast-on edge, ending after working a WS row.

Body

Change to larger needles. Work the pattern stitches as follows:

Row 1 (RS): K2, p13 (12, 13, 14, 15), k17 (21, 21, 21, 21) for center panel, p13 (12, 13, 14, 15), k2.

Note: In subsequent rows, maintain this pattern of stockinette stitch over stockinette and reverse stockinette stitch over reverse stockinette. Always keep 2 stitches in stockinette stitch at the end of each row, keep center 17 (21, 21, 21, 21) stitches in stockinette stitch, and keep the remaining stitches in reverse stockinette stitch.

Work 8 (6, 4, 4, 4) rows in pattern as established, ending after working a WS row.

As for Back, make 1 fully fashioned increase at each end of the row in purl on next row, and make 1 fully fashioned increase at each end every 4th row 0 (0, 2, 6, 14) times, every 6th row 0 (11, 14, 11, 5) times, then every 8th row 12 (3, 0, 0, 0) times—73 (79, 85, 89, 95) stitches.

Work even until the piece measures 16½ (16, 15½, 15, 14½)" [42 (40.5, 39.5, 38, 37)cm] from the edging.

Shape Cap

Next 2 rows: Bind off 5 (6, 6, 7, 7) stitches, work in pattern as established—63 (67, 73, 75, 81) stitches.

Next 0 (0, 0, 2, 2) rows: Bind off 3 stitches, work in pattern as established.

Next 2 rows: Bind off 2 stitches, work in pattern as established—59 (63, 69, 65, 71) stitches.

Decrease 1 stitch (with fully fashioned decreases) at the beginning and end of the next RS row, then every other row 15 (15, 16, 17, 17) times more—27 (31, 35, 29, 35) stitches.

Work in pattern as established, binding off 2 stitches at the beginning of the next 2 (2, 4, 4, 4) rows, then 3 stitches at the beginning of the next 2 (2, 2, 0, 2) rows.

Bind off the remaining 17 (21, 21, 21, 21) stitches.

Finishing
Block pieces to measurements.
Using a yarn needle, sew shoulder seams.

Collar
With RS facing and circular needle, beginning at center front neck, pick up and knit 35 (35, 36, 36, 37) stitches along Right Front neck, 51 (51, 53, 53, 55) stitches along Back neck, and 35 (35, 36, 36, 37) stitches along Left Front neck—121 (121, 125, 125, 129) stitches. Do not join.
Work back and forth in Seed Stitch for 3" [7.5cm] from the picked-up stitches.
Bind off loosely in Seed Stitch.
Sew Sleeves into armholes.
Sew side and Sleeve seams.
Sew buttons onto center Front, evenly spaced.

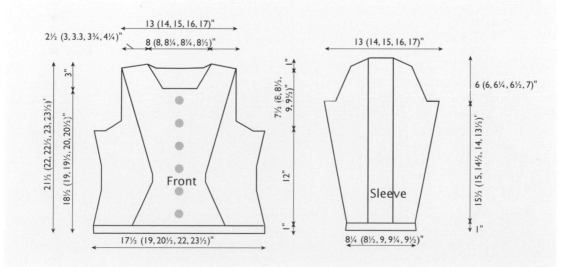

FLIRTY TOP

by Sally Melville

This garment can fit you perfectly, whether you want to increase the differentiation between bust and waist or show off your curves just the way they are. Uninterrupted coverage enhances the bust, while waist shaping and ruffling over the hips accentuate all the right places for a flirty look that flatters.

Skill Level
Intermediate

Sizes
XS (S, M, L, XL)

Finished Measurements
Bust: 34 (39, 43, 48, 53)" [86 (99, 109, 122, 134.5)cm]
Waist: 27½ (32, 36½, 41, 45½)" [70 (81, 92.5, 104, 115.5)cm]
Length (at center back, including ruffle): 24 (25, 25½, 26½, 27½)" [61 (63.5, 64.5, 67, 70)cm]
Length (at sides, including ruffle): 21 (21½, 22, 22½, 23)" [53 (54.5, 56, 57, 58)cm]
Waist length: 16½ (17, 17½, 18, 18½)" [42 (43, 44, 45.5. 47)cm]
Shoulder width: 14½ (14½, 15, 15, 15½)" [37 (37, 38, 38, 39.5)cm]
Sleeve length (including ruffle): 24 (24½, 26, 27½, 28½)" [61 (62, 66, 69.5, 72)cm]

Materials
630 (700, 770, 850, 910) yd [570 (630, 695, 765, 820)m] / 6 (6, 7, 7, 8) skeins Prism Pebbles (100% nylon, each approximately 2 oz [60g] and 123 yd [111m]), in color Smoke (MC), (4) medium/worsted weight

520 (575, 635, 690, 750) yd [470 (520, 570, 620, 675)m] / 6 (6, 7, 8, 8) skeins of Prism Tulle (100% nylon, each approximately 1 oz [30g] and 96 yd [86m]), in color Smoke (CC), (4) medium/worsted weight
1 Pair size 8 [5mm] needles, or size needed to obtain gauge
1 Pair size 6 [4mm] needles
1 Pair size 10 [6mm] needles
Stitch holder
Yarn needle

Gauge
14 stitches and 26 rows (13 garter ridges) = 4" [10cm] over garter stitch using size 8 [5mm] needles and MC

Pattern Notes
This garment is hourglass-shaped. The MC side seams can match your natural waist length, and the ruffle can fall to your ideal length for a Midlength Sweater at the side (page 11).
The main pieces are knit in MC and in garter stitch, so there is no right or wrong side until the ruffle is attached.
The ruffle is added after knitting the body pieces and is worked down, in reverse stockinette (purl on RS, knit on WS).

Instructions

Back
With middle-size needles and MC, e-wrap cast on 8 (12, 16, 20, 24) stitches.
Knit 1 row.
*E-wrap cast on 2 stitches, knit to end; repeat from * 19 (21, 23, 25, 27) times more—48 (56, 64, 72, 80) stitches.
Knit 8 rows even.
Increase row: K1, kf&b, knit to last 2 stitches, kf&b, k1.
Knit 7 rows even.
Repeat the last 8 rows 5 times more—60 (68, 76, 84, 92) stitches.
Work even in garter stitch until side measures 8½" [21.5cm]. (Shorten or lengthen the Back Waist length here, page 12.)

Shape Armholes
Next 2 rows: Bind off 2 (3, 4, 5, 6) stitches, work in pattern as established—56 (62, 68, 74, 80) stitches.
Decrease row: K1, skp, knit to last 3 stitches, k2tog, k1.
Next row: Knit 1 row.
Repeat the last 2 rows 2 (5, 7, 10, 12) times more—50 (50, 52, 52, 54) stitches. (Adjust the Shoulder width here, page 15.)
Work even in garter stitch until armhole measures 7 (7½, 8, 8½, 9)" [17.5 (19, 20.5, 21.5, 23)cm].

Shape Back Right Shoulder and Neck

Bind off 3 (3, 4, 4, 4) stitches, knit to 8 (8, 8, 8, 9) stitches on right needle. Slip the remaining 39 (39, 40, 40, 41) stitches onto a stitch holder. Turn.

Row 1: Slip 1 purlwise wyif, bind off 1 stitch at neck edge, knit to end.

Bind off 3 (3, 3, 3, 4) stitches at armhole edge.

Row 3: Slip 1 purlwise wyif, bind off 1 stitch at neck edge, knit to end.

Bind off remaining 3 stitches.

Shape Back Left Shoulder and Neck

Slip 39 (39, 40, 40, 41) stitches from the holder back onto the working needle.

Bind off 28 stitches at neck edge, knit to end.

Set-up row: Bind off 3 (3, 4, 4, 4) stitches at armhole edge, knit to end.

Work as for Shape Right Shoulder and Back Neck.

Add Ruffle

Choose the RS of the Back piece. With RS facing and the smallest needles and CC, pick up and knit as follows:

1 stitch for every cast-on stitch and 1 stitch for every 2-row step (between cast-on stitches)—approximately 68 (78, 88, 98, 108) stitches.

Next row (WS): Knit.

Increase row (RS): [K1, yo, k1] in every stitch across the row—approximately 204 (234, 264, 294, 324) stitches.

Beginning with a WS (knit row), work in reverse stockinette until the ruffle measures ¾" [2cm] from the picked-up stitches.

Change to the middle-size needles. Work even in reverse stockinette for 4 rows more.

Change to largest needles. Work even in reverse stockinette until the ruffle measures 4½" [11.5cm] from the picked-up stitches, ending after working a WS (knit row). (Shorten or lengthen the Finished Garment length here, page **12**.)

Cut CC.

Next row (RS): With MC, knit.

Bind off all stitches knitwise.

Front

Work as for Back until armhole measures 6 (6½, 7, 7½, 8)" [15 (16.5, 17.5, 19, 20.5)cm].

Shape Front Right Shoulder and Neck

Knit to 11 (11, 12, 12, 13) stitches on right needle. Place remaining 39 (39, 40, 40, 41) stitches on holder. Turn.

Row 1: Slip 1 purlwise wyif, bind off 1 stitch at neck edge, knit to end.

Row 2: Knit.

Row 3: Slip 1 purlwise wyif, bind off 1 stitch at neck edge, knit to end—9 (9, 10, 10, 11) stitches. Continuing to slip 1 purlwise at neck edge, knit even until armhole measures same length as Back.

Bind off 3 (3, 4, 4, 4) stitches at armhole edge.

Next row: Slip 1 purlwise wyif, knit to end.

Bind off 3 (3, 3, 3, 4) stitches at armhole edge.

Next row: Slip 1 purlwise wyif, knit to end.

Bind off remaining 3 stitches.

Shape Front Left Shoulder and Neck

Slip the 39 (39, 40, 40, 41) stitches from the stitch holder back onto the working needle.

Bind off 28 stitches at neck edge, knit to end.

Knit 1 row.

Work as for Shape Right Shoulder and Front Neck.

Add Ruffle

Work as for Back.

Sleeve (Make 2)

With middle-size needles and MC, e-wrap cast on 28 (30, 34, 38, 38) stitches.

Knit 8 rows.

Increase row: K1, kf&b, knit to last 2 stitches, kf&b, k1.

Knit 7 (5, 5, 3, 3) rows even.

Repeat the last 8 (6, 6, 4, 4) rows 6 (7, 8, 10, 13) times more—42 (46, 52, 60, 66) stitches.

Work even until piece measures 8½ (9, 9½, 10, 10)" [21.5 (23, 24, 25.5, 25.5)cm]. (Shorten or lengthen the Sleeve length here, page **13**.)

Shape Cap

Next 2 rows: Bind off 2 (3, 4, 5, 6) stitches, knit to end of row—38 (40, 44, 50, 54) stitches.

Decrease row: K1, skp, knit to last 3 stitches, k2tog, k1.

Knit 3 rows even.

Repeat the last 4 rows twice more—32 (34, 38, 44, 48) stitches.

Decrease row: K1, skp, knit to last 3 stitches, k2tog, k1.

Next row: Knit 1 row.

Repeat the last 2 rows 7 (8, 10, 13, 15) times more—16 stitches.

Next 2 rows: Bind off 2 stitches, knit to end. Bind off the remaining 12 stitches.

Add Ruffle

Choose the RS of the Sleeve piece. With RS facing, smallest needle and CC, pick up and knit 1 stitch for every cast-on stitch—28 (30, 34, 38, 38) stitches.

Next row (WS): *K1, kf&b; repeat from * to end—42 (45, 51, 57, 57) stitches.

Increase row (RS): [K1, yo, k1] in every stitch across the row—126 (135, 153, 171, 171) stitches.

Beginning with a WS (knit) row, work in reverse stockinette until the ruffle measures ¾" [2cm] from the picked-up stitches.

Change to middle-size needles. Work even in reverse stockinette for 4 rows more.

Change to largest needles. Work even in reverse stockinette until the ruffle measures 4" [10cm] from the picked-up stitches. End after working a WS (knit) row. Cut CC yarn.
Next row (RS): With MC, knit.
Bind off all stitches knitwise.

Finishing

Use a yarn needle and CC for all sewing.
Sew shoulder seams.
Sew Sleeves into armholes.
Sew side and Sleeve seams.
Sew ruffle seams.
Note: If the lower edges of the ruffles roll under, try one of these ideas: Steam gently, without pressing the ruffle. Or, wet the edges of all the ruffles, pin the ruffle edges together (Back ruffles to Front ruffles), and let dry.

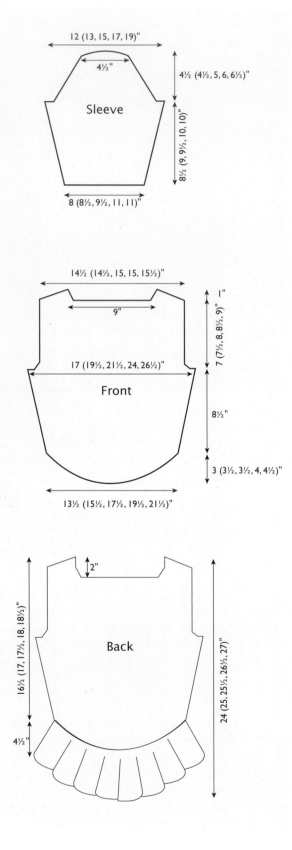

CORDED SWEATER

by Berta Karapetyan

The waist of this sweater is designed with somewhat of a close fit, so add ease there if you need it. The sweater should feel comfortable but have a sleek look; an I-cord–less cording technique creates chic vertical lines that have a nice slimming effect.

Skill Level
Experienced

Sizes
XS (S, M, L, XL)

Finished Measurements
Bust: 32 (35, 38, 41, 44)" [81 (89, 96.5, 104, 112)cm]
Length: 21 (21½, 22, 22½, 23)" [53 (54.5, 56, 57, 58.5)cm]
Upper arm: 11 (12, 13, 14, 15)" [28 (30.5, 33, 35.5, 38)cm]

Materials
770 (847, 924, 1078, 1155) yd [700 (770, 840, 980, 1050)m] / 10 (11, 12, 14, 15) balls
Karabella Margrite Bulky (80% extra fine merino wool, 20% cashmere, each approximately 1¾ oz [50g] and 77 yd [70m]), in color #16 Putty, (5) bulky weight
1 Pair size 10½ [6.5mm] needles, or size needed to obtain gauge
1 Size 10 [6mm] circular needle, 16" [40cm] long
1 Size 7 [4.5mm] circular needle, 16" [40cm] long
Stitch markers
Cable needle
Stitch holders
Yarn needle

Gauge
14 stitches and 21 rows = 4" [10cm] over stockinette stitch using size 10½ [6.5mm] needles

Stitch Glossary
3-st SLR (3-stitch slanted right crossing): Slip 2 stitches onto cable needle and hold to back, k1, k2 from cable needle.
3-st SLRD (3-stitch slanted right crossing with decrease): Slip 2 stitches onto cable needle and hold to back, k1, k2tog from cable needle.
3-st SLRI (3-stitch slanted right crossing with increase): Slip 2 stitches onto cable needle and hold to back, k1, M1, k2 from cable needle.
3-st SLRPD (3-stitch slanted right crossing with decrease on WS): Slip 1 stitch onto cable needle and hold to back, p2tog, p1 from cable needle.

3-st SLL (3-stitch slanted left crossing): Slip 1 stitch onto cable needle and hold to front, k2, k1 from cable needle.
3-st SLLD (3-stitch slanted left crossing with decrease): Slip 1 stitch onto cable needle and hold to front, ssk, k1 from cable needle.
3-st SLLI (3-stitch slanted left crossing with increase): Slip 1 stitch onto cable needle and hold to front, k2, M1, k1 from cable needle.
3-st SLLPD (3-stitch slanted left crossing with decrease on WS): Slip 2 stitches onto cable needle and hold to front, p1, p2tog from cable needle.
4-st CC (4-stitch cord crossing): Slip 3 stitches onto cable needle and hold to front, k1 from left-hand needle, slip 2 stitches from cable needle back to left-hand needle, leave last stitch on cable needle and hold to back, k2 from left-hand needle, k1 from cable needle.

Instructions

Back

With the size 10½ straight needles, cast on 65 (70, 75, 80, 85) stitches.

Row 1 (RS): K15 (17, 19, 21, 23), place marker, 4-st CC, k27 (28, 29, 30, 31), place marker, 4-st CC, k15 (17, 19, 21, 23). (**Note:** Slip markers in every row.)

Row 2 and all WS rows: Purl.

Rows 3, 7, and 11: Knit to 1st marker, slip marker, 4-st CC, knit to 2nd marker, slip marker, 4-st CC, knit to end.

Row 5: Knit to 3 stitches before 1st marker, 3-st SLR, slip marker, 4-st CC, 3-st SLL, knit to 3 stitches before 2nd marker, 3-st SLR, slip marker, 4-st CC, 3-st SLL, knit to end.

Row 9: Knit to 3 stitches before 1st marker, 3-st SLRD, slip marker, 4-st CC, 3-st SLLD, knit to 3 stitches before 2nd marker, 3-st SLRD, slip marker, 4-st CC, 3-st SLLD, knit to end—61 (66, 71, 76, 81) stitches.

Row 12: Work Row 2.

Next 16 rows: Repeat Rows 5–12 twice more—53 (58, 63, 68, 73) stitches.

Rows 29 and 33: Work Row 5.

Rows 31 and 35: Work Row 3.

Row 37: Knit to 3 stitches before 1st marker, 3-st SLRI, slip marker, 4-st CC, 3-st SLLI, knit to 3 stitches before 2nd marker, 3-st SLRI, slip marker, 4-st CC, 3-st SLLI, knit to end—57 (62, 67, 72, 77) stitches.

Rows 39, 43, and 47: Work Row 3.

Rows 41 and 45: Work Row 5.

Next 24 rows: Repeat Rows 37–48 twice more—65 (70, 75, 80, 85) stitches.

Row 73: Work Row 37—69 (74, 79, 84, 89) stitches.

Row 75: Work Row 3.

Shape Armholes

Row 77 (RS): Bind off 3 (3, 3, 4, 4) stitches, work Row 5—66 (71, 76, 80, 85) stitches.

Row 78: Bind off 3 (3, 3, 4, 4) stitches, purl to end—63 (68, 73, 76, 81) stitches.

Row 79: K2, ssk, knit to 1st marker, slip marker, 4-st CC, knit to 2nd marker, slip marker, 4-st CC, knit to last 4 stitches, k2tog, k2—61 (66, 71, 74, 79) stitches.

Row 81: K2, ssk, knit to 3 stitches before 1st marker, 3-st SLR, slip marker, 4-st CC, 3-st SLL, knit to 3 stitches before 2nd marker, 3-st

SLR, slip marker, 4-st CC, 3-st SLL, knit to last 4 stitches, k2tog, k2—59 (64, 69, 72, 77) stitches.

Row 82: Work Row 2.

Repeat Rows 79–82 1 (1, 2, 2, 2) times more—55 (60, 61, 64, 69) stitches.

Sizes XS (M, L) Only

Next row (RS): Knit to 1st marker, slip marker, 4-st CC, knit to 2nd marker, slip marker, 4-st CC, knit to end.

Next row: Purl.

Next row (RS): Knit to 3 stitches before 1st marker, 3-st SLR, slip marker, 4-st CC, 3-st SLL, knit to 3 stitches before 2nd marker, 3-st SLR, slip marker, 4-st CC, 3-st SLL, knit to end.

Next row: Purl.

Repeat last 4 rows until armhole measures 6½ (7½, 8)" [16.5 (19, 20)cm].

Sizes S and XL Only

Next row (RS): Work Row 79—(58 [67] stitches).

Next row: Purl.

Next row (RS): Knit to 3 stitches before 1st marker, 3-st SLR, slip marker, 4-st CC, 3-st SLL, knit to 3 stitches before 2nd marker, 3-st SLR, slip marker, 4-st CC, 3-st SLL, knit to end.

Next row: Purl.

Next row (RS): Knit to 1st marker, slip marker, 4-st CC, knit to 2nd marker, slip marker, 4-st CC, knit to end.

Next row: Purl.

Repeat last 4 rows until armhole measures 7 (8½)" [18 (21.5)cm].

Shape Shoulders

Next 2 rows: Bind off 6 (7, 7, 7, 8) stitches, work in pattern as established—43 (44, 47, 50, 51).

Next 2 rows: Bind off 6 (6, 7, 7, 7) stitches, work in pattern as established—31 (32, 33, 36, 37).

Next 2 rows: Bind off 6 (6, 6, 7, 7) stitches, work in pattern as established. Slip the remaining 19 (20, 21, 22, 23) stitches onto a stitch holder for the back neck.

Front

Work as for Back until armhole measures 5 (5½, 6, 6½, 7)" [12.5 (14, 15, 16.5, 18)cm]—55 (58, 61, 64, 67) stitches.

Shape Neck

Decrease row (RS): Work 21 (22, 23, 24, 25) stitches as established, k2tog, k1, place next 7 (8, 9, 10, 11) stitches on stitch holder for front, join 2nd ball of yarn, k1, ssk, work 21 (22, 23, 24, 25) stitches as established—23 (24, 25, 26, 27) stitches on each side.

Working both sides at once, repeat this decrease row every other row 5 times more—18 (19, 20, 21, 22) stitches on each side.

AT THE SAME TIME, when armhole measures 6½ (7, 7½, 8, 8½)" [15 (16.5, 18, 20, 21.5)cm], shape shoulders as for Back.

Sleeve (Make 2)

Cast on 33 (34, 35, 36, 37) stitches.

Work in stockinette stitch, increasing 1 stitch at the beginning and end of the following rows:

Size XS Only
Rows 31, 57, and 83—39 stitches.

Size S Only
Rows 21, 41, 61, and 81—42 stitches.

Size M Only
Rows 11, 27, 43, 59, and 75—45 stitches.

Size L Only
Rows 11, 25, 39, 53, 67, and 81—48 stitches.

Size XL Only
Rows 11, 23, 35, 47, 59, 71, and 83—51 stitches.

For All Sizes
Work even in stockinette stitch until the piece measures 18" [46cm] from the beginning.

Shape Cap

Rows 1 and 2: Bind off 3 (3, 3, 4, 4) stitches, work in stockinette stitch to end—33 (36, 39, 40, 43) stitches.

Decrease row (RS): K2, 3-st SLRD, knit to last 5 stitches, 3-st SLLD, k2—31 (34, 37, 38, 41) stitches.

Work in stockinette stitch, repeating this decrease row on the following rows:

Size XS Only
Rows 7, 11, 15, and 19—23 stitches.

Sizes S and M Only
Rows 7, 11, 15, 19, and 23—24 (27) stitches.

Size L Only
Rows 7, 11, 15, 19, 23, and 27—26 stitches.

Size XL Only
Rows 7, 11, 15, 19, 23, 27, and 31—27 stitches.

Size XS Only
Rows 20, 22, and 24: P2, 3-st SLLPD, purl to last 5 stitches, 3-st SLRPD, p2.
Rows 21, 23, and 25: Work Row 3—11 stitches.

Size S Only
Rows 24, 26, and 28: P2, 3-st SLLPD, purl to last 5 stitches, 3-st SLRPD, p2.
Rows 25, 27, and 29: Work Row 3—12 stitches.

Size M Only
Rows 24, 26, 28, and 30: P2, 3-st SLLPD, purl to last 5 stitches, 3-st SLRPD, p2—13 stitches (after Row 30).
Rows 25, 27, and 29: Work Row 3—13 stitches.

Size L Only
Rows 28, 30, and 32: P2, 3-st SLLPD, purl to last 5 stitches, 3-st SLRPD, p2.
Rows 29, 31, and 33: Work Row 3—14 stitches.

Size XL Only
Rows 32, 34, and 36: P2, 3-st SLLPD, purl to last 5 stitches, 3-st SLRPD, p2.
Rows 33, 35, and 37: Work Row 3—15 stitches.

For All Sizes
Bind off remaining 11 (12, 13, 14, 15) stitches.

Finishing

Using a yarn needle, sew shoulder seams.

Collar

With RS facing and size 10 [6mm] circular needle, knit across 19 (20, 21, 22, 23) stitches from back neck holder, pick up and knit 14 stitches along left neck edge, knit across 7 (8, 9, 10, 11) stitches from front neck holder, pick up and knit 14 stitches along right neck edge—54 (56, 58, 60, 62) stitches. Join in round and work in stockinette stitch (knit every round) for 4" [10cm]. Change to size 7 [4.5mm] circular needle and purl next 2 rounds. Bind off loosely.
Sew Sleeves into armholes.
Sew side and Sleeve seams.

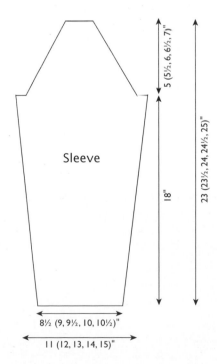

Sleeve

5 (5½, 6, 6½, 7)"

18"

23 (23½, 24, 24½, 25)"

8½ (9, 9½, 10, 10½)"

11 (12, 13, 14, 15)"

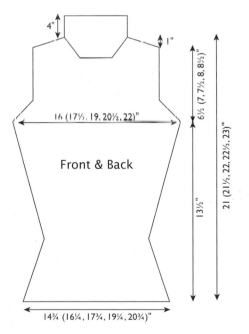

Front & Back

4"

1"

16 (17½, 19, 20½, 22)"

6½ (7, 7½, 8, 8½)"

13½"

21 (21½, 22, 22½, 23)"

14¾ (16¼, 17¾, 19¼, 20¾)"

VINTAGE "SWEATER GIRL" CROPPED SWEATER

by Lily Chin

Evocative of the illustrations of Alberto Vargas pin-up girls in the 40s and 50s, this pullover is extremely flattering. The wide V-neck draws attention upward toward the face. Add a bit of elastic thread to the neck and bind off loosely to have the option of wearing it off the shoulders.

Skill Level
Intermediate

Sizes
S (M, L, 1X, 2X)

Finished Measurements
Bust: 34 (38, 43, 47½, 52)" [86.5 (96.5, 109, 120.5, 132)cm]
Waist: 29 (33, 37, 42½, 47)" [73.5 (84, 94, 108, 119.5)cm]
Length: 16 (16½, 16½, 17, 17)" [40.5 (42, 42, 43, 43)cm]
Upper arm: 13½ (14, 14½, 15, 15½)" [34 (35.5, 37, 38, 39.5)cm]

Materials
1071 (1071, 1224, 1377, 1530) yd (980 [980, 1120, 1260, 1400]m) / 7 (7, 8, 9, 10) balls Lily Chin Signature Collection Tribeca (43% wool, 25% mohair, 17% viscose, 15% nylon, each approximately 1¾ oz [50g] and 153 yd [140m]), in color #1268 Pink, ⑤ bulky/chunky weight
1 Pair size 7 (4.5mm) needles
1 Pair size 9 (5.5mm) needles, or size needed to obtain gauge
1 Size 7 (4.5mm) circular needle, 16" [40cm] long
Yarn needle

Gauge
16 stitches and 24 rows = 4" (10cm) over stockinette stitch using size 9 (5.5mm) needles

Pattern Stitch
1x1 Rib (over a multiple of 2 stitches + 1)
Row 1 (RS): K1, *p1, k1; repeat from * to end.
Row 2: P1, *k1, p1; repeat from * to end.
Repeat Rows 1 and 2 for 1x1 Rib.

Instructions

Back
With smaller straight needles, cast on 59 (67, 77, 87, 95) stitches.
Work in 1x1 Rib for 4" (10cm), ending after working a WS row.
Change to larger needles.
Work in stockinette stitch.
AT THE SAME TIME, shape the sides as follows:
Increase row (RS): K2, kf&b, knit to last 3 stitches, kf&b, k2.
Repeat increase row every 8th row 4 times more—69 (77, 87, 97, 105) stitches.
Work even until piece measures 12" (30.5cm) from the cast-on edge, ending after working a WS row.

Shape Raglan Armholes
Next 2 rows: Bind off 3 (4, 4, 4, 7) stitches, work in pattern as established—63 (69, 79, 89, 91) stitches.
Decrease row (RS): K2, k2tog, knit to last 4 stitches, ssk, k2.
Repeat decrease row every other row 0 (0, 8, 13, 13) times more, every 4th row 1 (6, 2, 0, 0) times, then every 6th row 3 (0, 0, 0, 0) times.
AT THE SAME TIME, when the armhole measures 1" (2.5cm), end with a WS row.

Shape Neck
Next row (RS): Work to center 3 stitches, join a 2nd ball of yarn, bind off center 3 stitches.

Working both sides at once, continue to shape raglan armholes.

AT THE SAME TIME, bind off at each neck edge as follows:

Size S Only
[3 stitches once, 2 stitches once, then 3 stitches once] 3 times.

Size M Only
[2 stitches once, then 3 stitches once] 5 times.

Size L Only
[3 stitches] 8 times, then 2 stitches once.

Size 1X Only
[2 stitches once, 3 stitches once, then 2 stitches once] 4 times.

Size 2X Only
[3 stitches once, 2 stitches once, then 3 stitches once] 3 times, 2 stitches once, then 3 stitches once.

For All Sizes
Fasten off last stitch each side.

Front
Work as for Back.

Sleeve (Make 2)
With smaller needles, cast on 37 (39, 41, 43, 45) stitches.

Work in 1x1 Rib for 3" (7.5cm), ending after working a WS row.

Work even in stockinette stitch until piece measures 13" (33cm) from cast-on edge, ending after working a WS row.

AT THE SAME TIME, work increases as follows:

Increase row (RS): K2, kf&b, knit to last 3 stitches, kf&b, k2.

Work increase row every 6th row 8 times more—55 (57, 59, 61, 63) stitches.

Shape Raglan Cap
Next 2 rows: Bind off 3 (4, 4, 4, 7) stitches, work in pattern as established—49 (49, 51, 53, 49) stitches.

Work decrease rows as for Back as follows:

Size S Only
[Every other row 3 times, then every 4th row once] twice, then every other row twice.

Size M Only
[Every other row twice, then every 4th row once] 3 times, then every other row once.

Size L Only
[Every other row 3 times, then every 4th row once] twice, then every other row 3 times.

Size 1X Only
[Every other row twice, then every 4th row once] 3 times, then every other row twice.

Size 2X Only
[Every 4th row once, then every other row once] 4 times, then every 4th row once.

For All Sizes
Work even on 29 (29, 29, 31, 31) stitches until cap measures 4 (4½, 4½, 5, 5)" [10 (11.5, 11.5, 12.5, 12.5)cm], ending after working a WS row. Bind off all stitches.

Finishing
Block pieces to measurements.

Using a yarn needle, sew raglan caps to raglan armholes.

Sew side and Sleeve seams.

Neck Band
With RS facing and smaller circular needle, pick up and knit 63 (65, 67, 69, 71) stitches across Back neck, 27 (27, 27, 29, 29) stitches across top of one sleeve, 63 (65, 67, 69, 71) stitches across Front neck, and 27 (27, 27, 29, 29) stitches across top of other sleeve—180 (184, 188, 196, 200) stitches.

Place marker for the beginning of the round, and join stitches for working in the round.

Round 1: Work in 1x1 Rib across first 31 (32, 33, 34, 35) stitches, knit next stitch and mark as center stitch, [work in 1x1 Rib across next 44 (45, 46, 48, 49) stitches, knit next stitch and mark as center stitch] 3 times, work in 1x1 Rib across last 13 (13, 13, 14, 14) stitches.

Keeping center as knit stitches each round, work as follows:

Round 2: [Work in 1x1 Rib as established to within 2 stitches of center stitch, ssk, k1, k2tog] 4 times, work in pattern as established—172 (176, 180, 188, 192) stitches.

Round 3: Work in 1x1 Rib as established with knit stitches on either side of center knit stitches.

Round 4: [Work in 1x1 Rib as established to within 2 stitches of center stitch, ssp, k1, p2tog] 4

times, work in 1x1 Rib as established—164 (168, 172, 180, 184) stitches.

Round 5: Work in 1x1 Rib as established.
Repeat Rounds 2–5 for approximately 3" [7.5cm] with 8 fewer stitches every other round, ending after working Round 4.
Bind off loosely in 1x1 Rib.

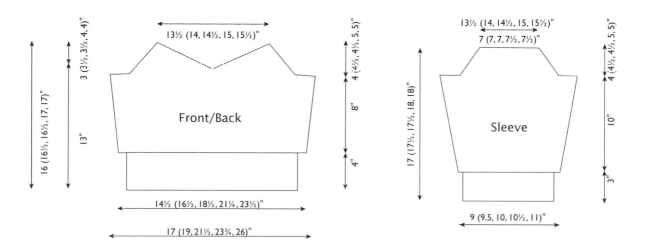

13½ (14, 14½, 15, 15½)"

3 (3½, 3½, 4, 4)"

16 (16½, 16½, 17, 17)"

13"

Front/Back

14½ (16½, 18½, 21¼, 23½)"

17 (19, 21½, 23¾, 26)"

4 (4½, 4½, 5, 5)"

8"

4"

13½ (14, 14½, 15, 15½)"

7 (7, 7, 7½, 7½)"

4 (4½, 4½, 5, 5)"

17 (17½, 17½, 18, 18)"

10"

3"

Sleeve

9 (9.5, 10, 10½, 11)"

chapter three

CARDIGANS AND COVER-UPS

From Monday morning to a lazy weekend afternoon, a hand-knit cover-up always fits the bill. Some days, you just want to throw on a comfortable, cozy hoodie—and Sally Melville's Sophisticated Hoodie does all that, while still looking polished. Other times, you need a dressier piece—that where Berta Karapetyan's elegant Ruffled Cardigan comes in. With these patterns, you'll have just the right sweater for every occasion, every day of the week.

SEASHELL CARDI

by Berta Karapetyan

The body of this merino wool shrug is worked in one piece, but the real magic lies in its shaping. Figuring out how to put on the piece for the first time may be a bit of a puzzler, but once you slip into its cozy contours, you'll love the snug, slimming fit.

Skill Level
Experienced

Sizes
S/M (L/XL)

Finished Measurements
Width (folded in half): 22 (24½)" [56 (62)cm]
Length: 21 (21½)" [53 (54.5)cm]
Upper arm: 13 (13½)" [33 (34)cm]

Materials
1862 (2058) yd [1653 (1827)m] / 19 (21) balls Karabella Aurora 8 (100% extra fine merino wool, each approximately 1¾ oz [50g] and 98 yd [90m]), in color #35 Pale Gray, (4) medium/worsted weight
1 Pair size 7 [4.5mm] needles, or size needed to obtain gauge
1 Size 7 [4.5mm] circular needle, 40" [101.5cm] long
Stitch markers

Gauge
26 stitches and 28 rows = 4" [10cm] over slightly stretched 2x2 rib (page 134) using size 7 [4.5mm] needles

Instructions

Sleeve (Make 2)
With straight needles, cast on 78 (82) stitches.
Row 1 (RS): K2, *p2, k2; repeat from * to end.
Row 2: P2, *k2, p2; repeat from * to end.
Repeat these 2 rows until piece measures 18½" [47cm] from the cast-on edge.

Shape Front
Place marker to indicate beginning of RS row. Work in established pattern with decreases as follows:

Size S/M Only
Decrease 1 stitch at the beginning (after the 1st stitch) of each RS row and at the end (before the last stitch) of each WS row for 52 rows. Omit decrease on Rows 2, 6, 10, 14, 18, 22, 26, 30, 34, 38, 42, and 50—38 stitches.

Size L/XL Only
Decrease 1 stitch at the beginning (after the 1st stitch) of each RS row and at the end of each WS row (before the last stitch) for 60 rows. Omit decrease on Rows 2, 4, 8, 10, 14, 16, 20, 22, 26, 28, 32, 36, 38, 40, 44, 48, 52, 54, 58, and 60—42 stitches.

For All Sizes
Work even for 4½ (5½)" [11 (14)cm] from last decrease row.
Work in established pattern with increases as follows:

Size S/M Only
Increase 1 stitch at the beginning (after the 1st stitch) of each RS row and at the end (before the last stitch) of each WS row for 52 rows. Omit increase on Rows 2, 6, 10, 14, 18, 22, 26, 30, 34, 38, 42, and 50—78 stitches.

Size L/XL Only
Increase 1 stitch at the beginning (after the 1st stitch) of each RS row and at the end (before the last stitch) of each WS row for 60 rows. Omit increase on Rows 2, 4, 8, 10, 14, 16, 20, 22, 26, 28, 32, 36, 38, 40, 44, 48, 52, 54, 58, and 60—82 stitches.

For All Sizes
Bind off all remaining stitches. Sew Sleeve seams.

Body
Note: The Body is worked in the round as one piece. Place markers exactly as indicated below to guarantee that the finished garment has a symmetrical look.

With WS of the shrug facing, place 8 markers around the opening, beginning as follows:

1st marker: In the middle of Back neck, between the 2 Sleeves.

2nd marker: In the middle of Right Front raglan line.

3rd marker: In the middle of Left Front raglan line.

4th marker: At the end of seam of Right Sleeve (beginning of Right Front raglan).

5th marker: At the end of seam of Left Sleeve (beginning of Left Front raglan).

6th marker: In the middle of lower Back.

7th marker: Centered between the 4th and 6th markers.

8th marker: Centered between the 5th and 6th markers.

With RS facing and circular needle, starting at 4th marker, pick up and knit 32 (36) stitches between each marker—256 (288) stitches. Join in the round, place marker on the needle to indicate beginning of rounds.

Round 1: Place marker, k2, place marker, M1, [k2, p2] 7 (8) times, k2, [M1, place marker, p2, place marker, M1, (k2, p2) 7 (8) times, k2] 3 times, [M1, place marker, k2, place marker, M1, (k2, p2) 7 (8) times, k2] 4 times, M1—272 (304) stitches.

Slipping markers every round, work as follows:

Rounds 2-4: Work stitches as they appear, purling all added stitches.

Round 5: Slip marker, k2, slip marker, M1, p1, [k2, p2] 7 (8) times, k2, [p1, M1, slip marker, p2, slip marker, M1, p1, (k2, p2) 7 (8) times, k2] 3 times, [p1, M1, slip marker, k2, slip marker, M1, p1, (k2, p2) 7 (8) times, k2], 4 times, p1, M1—288 (320) stitches.

Rounds 6-8: Work Rounds 2-4.

Round 9: Slip marker, k2, slip marker, M1, p2, [k2, p2] 7 (8) times, k2, [p2, M1, slip marker, p2, slip marker, M1, p2, (k2, p2) 7 (8) times, k2] 3 times, [p2, M1, slip marker, k2, slip marker, M1, p2, (k2, p2) 7 (8) times, k2] 4 times, p2, M1—304 (336) stitches.

Rounds 10-12: Work stitches as they appear, knitting all added stitches.

Round 13: Slip marker, k2, slip marker, M1, k1, p2, [k2, p2] 7 (8) times, k2, [p2, k1, M1, slip marker, p2, slip marker, M1, k1, p2, (k2, p2) 7 (8) times, k2] 3 times, [p2, k1, M1, slip marker, k2, slip marker, M1, k1, p2, (k2, p2) 7 (8) times, k2] 4 times, p2, k1, M1—320 (352) stitches.

Rounds 14-16: Work Rounds 10-12.

Repeat Rounds 1-16 five times more—640 (672) stitches.

Bind off loosely.

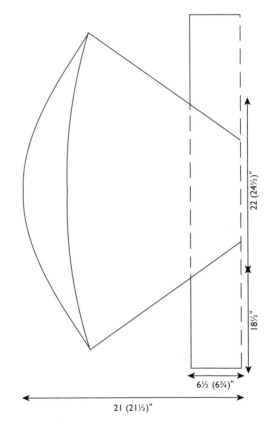

MRS. DARCY CARDIGAN

by Mary Weaver

A wardrobe staple gets a flirty, fitted update featuring raglan shoulders that balance out your top half and enhance an ultra-feminine hourglass shape. The deep scoop neck is the perfect way to show off a beautiful blouse.

Skill Level
Intermediate

Sizes
XS (S, M, L, XL)

Finished Measurements
Bust (closed): 30 (34, 38, 42, 46) [76 (86, 96.5, 106.5, 117)cm]
Length: Adjustable. This sweater is knit from the bottom up, so join the sleeves when it is long enough to fit.
Upper arm: 10 (10½, 11, 12, 13½)" [25.5 (26.5, 28, 30.5, 34)cm]

Materials
735 (980, 1225, 1470, 1715) yd [672 (896, 1120, 1344, 1568)m] / 3 (4, 5, 6, 7) skeins Brown Sheep Company Nature Spun Worsted (100% wool, each approximately 3½ oz [100g] and 245 yd [224m]), in color #125 Goldenrod, (4) medium/worsted weight
1 Set of 5 size 9 [5.5mm] double-pointed needles

1 Size 9 [5.5mm] circular needle, 32" [81cm] long, or size needed to obtain gauge
Stitch markers
Scrap yarn for stitch holders
Yarn needle
Sewing needle
Sewing thread
4 Buttons, ¾" [19mm] wide

Gauge
16 stitches and 22 rows = 4" [10cm] over stockinette stitch using size 9 (5.5mm) needle

Pattern Stitch
Twisted Rib (over an even number of stitches)
Row 1 (RS): *K1tbl, p1*; repeat from * to end.
Row 2: *K1, p1*; repeat from * to end.
Repeat Rows 1 and 2 for Twisted Rib.

Instructions

Sleeve (Make 2)
With double-pointed needles, cast on 32 (34, 36, 40, 44) stitches and divide stitches evenly over 4 needles. Join, taking care not to twist stitches on needles, and place marker for beginning of rounds.
Work around in Twisted Rib as follows:
Next round: *K1tbl, p1; repeat from * around.
Next round: *K1, p1; repeat from * around.
Repeat these 2 rounds 10 times more.
Knit 6 rounds.
Increase round: K1, M1, knit to last stitch, M1, k1—34 (36, 38, 42, 46) stitches.

Repeat these 7 rounds 3 (3, 3, 3, 4) times more—40 (42, 44, 48, 54) stitches.
Work even in stockinette stitch until piece measures 16½ (17, 17, 17½, 17½)" [42 (43, 43, 44.5, 44.5)cm] from cast-on edge.
Next round: Knit to last 4 (5, 6, 7, 8) stitches; place the next 8 (10, 12, 14, 16) stitches onto scrap yarn for underarm and slip the remaining 32 (32, 32, 34, 38) stitches onto a stitch holder for Sleeve.
Cut yarn, leaving a 12" [30.5cm] tail. Set aside.

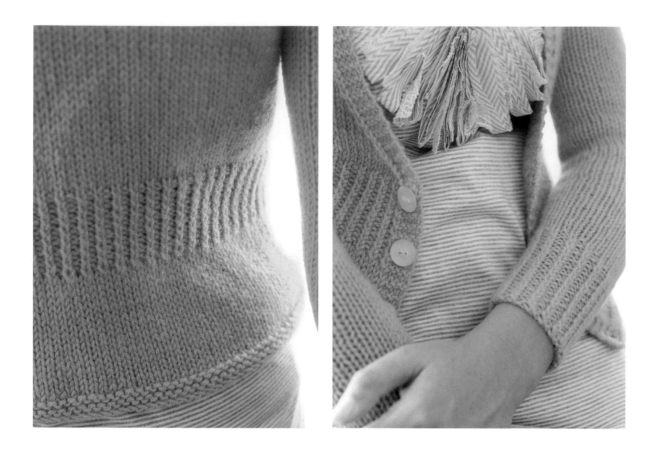

Body

With circular needle, cast on 124 (140, 156, 172, 188) stitches.

Next row (RS): K4 (right front band), place marker, knit to last 4 stitches, place marker, k4 (left front band).

Knit next row.

Buttonhole row (RS) K1, ssk, yo, knit to end.

Knit 1 row.

Next row (RS): K32 (36, 40, 44, 48), place marker, k60 (68, 76, 84, 92), place marker, knit to end.

Next row (WS): K4, purl to last 4 stitches, k4.

Keeping 4 stitches each side in garter stitch for front bands throughout, work remaining stitches in stockinette stitch and work even for 8 rows more.

Next row (RS); Work Buttonhole row.

Work even for 9 rows.

Waistband

Next row (RS): K4, slip marker, work in Twisted Rib to last 4 stitches, k4.

Work next row even as established.

Buttonhole row (RS) K1, ssk, yo, work in Twisted Rib to last 4 stitches, k4.

Work even for 11 rows.

Next (RS): Work Buttonhole row.

Next row (WS): K4, purl to last 4 stitches, k4.

Shape Neck

Decrease Row 1 (RS): K4, k2tog, knit to last 6 stitches, ssk, k4.

Decrease Row 2: K4, ssp, purl to last 6 stitches, p2tog, k4.

Repeat these 2 rows once more, then work Decrease Row 1 once—114 (130, 146, 162, 178) stitches.

Next row: K4, purl to last 4 stitches, k4.

Decrease Row 3 (RS): K4, k2tog, knit to last 6 stitches, ssk, k4.

Repeat last 2 rows 4 times more—104 (120, 136, 152, 168) stitches.

Work next 3 rows even.

Decrease Row 4 (RS): K4, k2tog, knit to last 6 stitches, ssk, k4.

Repeat last 4 rows once more—100 (116, 132, 148, 164) stitches.

Work even as established until body measures 8¾ (9, 9¼, 9½, 9¾)" [22 (23, 23.5, 24, 25)cm] from last row of ribbing, or until piece reaches to just below underarms when tried on with ribbing centered at waistline, ending after working a RS row.

Next row (WS): K4, slip marker, *purl to 4 (5, 6, 7, 8) stitches of next marker, purl next 8 (10, 12, 14, 16) stitches dropping marker, place these 8 (10, 12, 14, 16) stitches on scrap yarn for underarm; repeat from * once more, purl to last marker, slip marker, k4.

Join Body and Sleeves

Next row (RS): K4, slip marker, knit to underarm stitches, place marker, k32 (32, 32, 34, 38) stitches from 1st Sleeve holder, place marker, knit to next underarm stitches, place marker, k32 (32, 32, 34, 38) stitches from 2nd Sleeve holder, place marker, knit to last marker, slip marker, k4—148 (160, 172, 188, 208) stitches.

Yoke

Work even as established for 1" [2.5cm], ending after working a WS row.

Decrease row (RS): K4, slip marker, *knit to 3 stitches before next marker, ssk, k1, slip marker, k1, k2tog; repeat from * 3 times more, knit to end—140 (152, 164, 180, 200) stitches.

Next row: K4, purl to last 4 stitches, k4.

Repeat these last 2 rows 9 (10, 11, 12, 14) times more, then work the decrease row once more (dropping all markers on last row)—60 (64, 68, 76, 80) stitches.

Next row (WS): Knit.

Next row (RS): Ssk, knit to last 2 stitches, k2tog.

Repeat these last 2 rows twice more.

Bind off remaining 54 (58, 62, 70, 74) stitches.

Finishing

Transfer each group of underarm stitches from scrap yarn back to double-pointed needles. Join with corresponding stitches using a yarn needle and Kitchener Stitch, making sure to close any holes at each side of grafted seam.

Gently wet-block sweater to the measurements. Using a sewing needle and thread, sew on buttons.

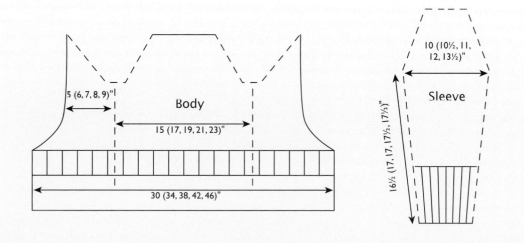

COZY MOSS SHRUG

by Berta Karapetyan

This adorable shrug knits up quickly thanks to its simple construction. Its 1x1 ribbing and graceful curves are easy to knit and flatter most figures—and its smart look complements outfits from dressy to casual. Nothing beats this sweater for its soft and cozy feel.

Skill Level
Intermediate

Sizes
S/M (L/XL)

Finished Measurements
Bust: 34 (38)" [86 (96.5)cm]
Length: 20 (20½)" [51 (52)cm]
Upper arm: 13 (14)" [33 (35.5)cm]

Materials
378 (432) yd [350 (400)m] / 7 (8) balls Karabella Puffy (100% merino wool, each approximately 3½ oz [100g] and 54 yd [50m]), in color #55 Moss Green, (6) super bulky/bulky weight
1 Pair size 15 [10mm] needles, or size needed to obtain gauge

Yarn needle

Gauge
10 stitches and 12 rows = 4" [10cm] over 1x1 Rib using size 15 [10mm] needles

Pattern Note
The shrug is worked in one piece from Right Sleeve to Left Sleeve.

Pattern Stitch
1x1 Rib (over a multiple of 2 stitches + 1)
Row 1 (RS). K1, *p1, k1; repeat from * to end
Row 2: P1, *k1, p1; repeat from * to end.
Repeat Rows 1 and 2 for 1x1 Rib.

Instructions

Shrug
Cast on 31 (33) stitches.
Work 40 rows in 1x1 Rib.
Row (increase) 41: (RS) K1, M1, work in 1x1 Rib to last stitch, M1, k1.
Work in pattern, repeating the increase on Rows 51, 55, 56, 57, 58, and 59—45 (47) stitches.
Row 60: Work in pattern to end of row, then cast on 15 stitches—60 (62) stitches.
Row 61: Work in pattern to end of row, then cast on 15 stitches—75 (77) stitches.
Rows 62-67 (62-69): Work even in pattern.
Row 68 (70): Work in pattern to last 3 stitches, decrease 1 stitch, k1—74 (76) stitches.
Row 69 (71): K1, decrease 1 stitch, work in pattern to end—73 (75) stitches.
Row 70 (72): Work in pattern to last 3 stitches, decrease 1 stitch, k1, cast on 16 (18) stitches—88 (92) stitches.

Work even in pattern for 16 rows more—86 (88) rows.
Row 87 (89): Bind off 44 (46) stitches for Front opening, work in pattern over 44 (46) stitches for Back.
Row 88 (90): Work 44 (46) stitches in pattern, cast on 44 (46) stitches for Front—88 (92) stitches.
Work even in pattern for 16 rows more—104 (106) rows.
Row 105 (107): Bind off 16 (18) stitches, k1, M1, work in pattern to end—73 (75) stitches.
Row 106 (108): Work in pattern to last 2 stitches, M1, k1—74 (76) stitches.
Row 107 (109): K1, M1, work in pattern to end—75 (77) stitches.
Rows 108-113 (110-115): Work in pattern.
Row 114 (116): Bind off 15 stitches, work in pattern to end—60 (62) stitches.

Row 115 (117): Bind off 15 stitches, work in pattern to end—45 (47) stitches.

Work in pattern as established, decreasing 1 stitch at the beginning and end of the next 5 rows—35 (37) stitches.

Work even in pattern for 4 rows more.

Row (decrease) 125 (127): Work in pattern, decreasing 1 stitch at the beginning and end of the row—33 (35) stitches.

Work in pattern, repeating last decrease row on row 134 (136)—31 (33) stitches.

Work even in pattern for 40 rows more.

Bind off all stitches.

Finishing

Pick up and knit 40 (44) stitches evenly along the bottom edge of the Back. Work in 1x1 Rib for 16 rows.

Bind off all stitches.

Using a yarn needle, sew Right Front Band to Right Front, connecting points A and B (see diagram below).

Sew Left Front Band to Left Front, connecting points C and D (see diagram below).

Sew side and Sleeve seams.

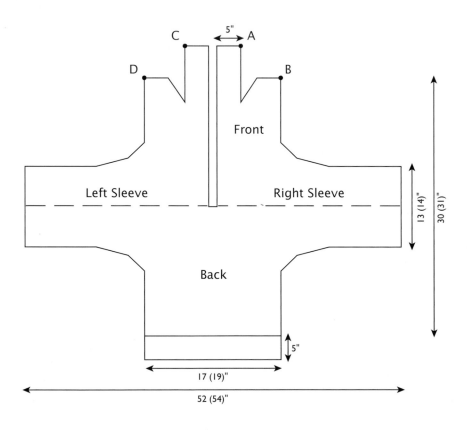

TWO-WAY SHRUG

by Caddy Melville Ledbetter

This shrug was developed for those times when you need some warmth but don't want to hide the outfit underneath. Cozy at the shoulders but loose everywhere else, this piece is ideal for highlighting the top of your hourglass figure.

Skill Level
Beginner

Sizes
XS/S (M/L, XL)

Finished Measurements
Bust (closed): 34 (39, 44)" [86 (98.5, 112)cm]
Length (at back, including collar): 17½ (20½, 25½)" [44.5 (52, 64.5)cm]

Materials
Lana Grossa Luxor (51% merino wool, 49% microfiber, each approximately 1¾ oz [50g] and 165 yd [150m], 🔳 medium/worsted weight 370 (430, 485) yd [335 (390, 435)m] / 3 (3, 3) balls in color #006 Silver (MC)
30 (35, 40) yd [27 (32, 36)m] / 1 (1, 1) ball in color #005 Charcoal (CC)

1 Pair size 10 [6mm] needles, or size needed to obtain gauge
1 Button, ½" [13mm] wide
1 Button, ¾" [20mm] wide
Yarn needle

Gauge
16 stitches and 24 rows = 4" [10cm] over stockinette stitch using size 10 [6mm] needles

Pattern Notes
This shrug is knit from the bottom up.
Work all increases as lifted increases.
To help get your bearings, remember that the top of your shrug does not have a border.
Because the stitch pattern is loosely knit, buttonholes are not needed; buttons easily fit through holes in the fabric.

Instructions

Shrug
With CC, cast on 126 (144, 162) stitches.
Work in 1x1 Rib (page **134**) for 3 rows.
With MC, knit 1 row, then purl 1 row.
Decrease row (RS): K1, skp, knit to last 3 stitches, k2tog, k1.
Work 3 (5, 7) rows even.
Repeat the last 4 (6, 8) rows 15 (13, 13) times more, ending after working 3 (5, 7) rows even—94 (116, 134) stitches.

Shape Collar
Increase row (RS): K1, kf&b in next stitch, knit to last 2 stitches, kf&b, k1.
Work 5 rows even.
Repeat the last 6 rows 5 times more, ending after working 5 rows even—106 (128, 146) stitches.
Bind off all stitches.

Finishing
Side Edgings
With RS facing and CC, pick up and knit 1 stitch for every row along entire side edge.
Work 1x1 Rib for 2 rows.
Bind off in ribbing pattern.
Repeat for the opposite side edge.

Assembly
Referring to the schematic, fold the shrug over to match points A and B. Using a yarn needle, sew the edges together toward points C and D for 1½" [3.8cm].
With RS facing, sew the large button onto the top left corner of the ribbed edge (as shown by the large circle on the schematic). Sew the smaller button onto the top right corner, ¾" [2cm] from the ribbed edge (as shown by the small circle on the schematic).

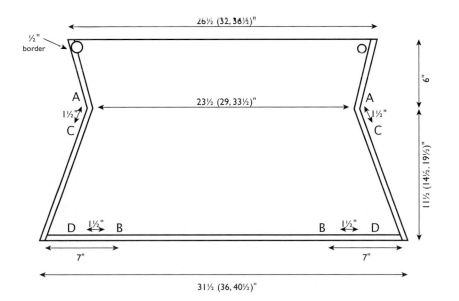

26½ (32, 38½)"

½"
border

6"

A

1½"

C

23½ (29, 33½)"

A

1½"

C

11½ (14½, 19½)"

D 1½" B

B 1½" D

7"

7"

31½ (36, 40½)"

CLASSIC SHIRT

by Sally Melville

This project is a great one to make on your path to becoming a more creative, more accomplished, or more successful knitter. The classic "button-down shirt" construction features shaping at the shoulders and waist as well as set-in armholes for a professional finish.

Skill Level
Intermediate

Sizes
S (M, L, 1X, 2X)

Finished Measurements
Bust (and hem): 36 (40, 44, 48, 52)" [91 (101, 111.5, 122, 132)cm]
Waist: 30 (34, 38, 42, 46)" [76 (86, 96.5, 106.5, 117)cm]
Length: 22½ (23, 23½, 24, 24½)" [57 (58, 59.5, 61, 62)cm]
Waist length: 16½ (17, 17½, 18, 18½)" [41.5 (43, 44, 45.5, 47)cm]
Shoulder width: 14" [35.5cm]
Sleeve length (with cuff extended): 31" (31½, 32, 32½, 33") [78.5 (80, 81, 82.5, 83.5)cm]

Materials
865 (960, 1060, 1150, 1250) yd [780 (865, 955, 1035, 1125)m] / 4 (5, 5, 5, 6) balls Needful Mohair Royal (80% kid mohair, 20% nylon, each approximately ⅞ oz [25g] and 235 yd [215m]), in color #1650 Off White, **(2)** fine/sport weight
or
1080 (1200, 1320, 1440, 1560) yd [970 (1080, 1200, 1320, 1440)m] / 4 (5, 5, 6, 6) skeins Louet Euroflax Sport Weight (100% linen, each approximately 3½ oz [100g] and 270 yd [246m]), in color #01 Champagne, **(2)** fine/sport weight
1 Pair size 6 [4mm] needles, or size needed to obtain gauge
1 Pair size 4 [3.5mm] needles
Stitch markers
Stitch holder
Yarn needle
Steam iron or garment steamer
10 Buttons, ⅜" [9mm] wide
2 Optional buttons (for turned-back cuffs)

Gauge
20 stitches and 28-30 rows = 4" [10cm] over stockinette stitch using larger needles (after steam-pressing)

Pattern Notes
This garment is hourglass-shaped, so it could fall between your ideal lengths for Short and Midlength Sweaters. The linen version is shown to the length written above, and the mohair version is 2" [5cm] longer. Adjust the Back Waist length (between the waist and the armhole) and the Finished Garment length (between the waist and the hem) as indicated on page 12.
The final measurements were 28 rows = 4" [10cm] for the linen version and 30 rows = 4" [10cm] for the mohair version. The pattern is written to accommodate either row gauge.
Neither I nor the yarn companies can explain why the heavier linen—which was knitted to a looser row gauge—took more yarn. But it definitely did!
Work all pieces in stockinette stitch unless otherwise indicated.
Work all increases as lifted increases.
The sleeves are long enough for the cuffs to be turned back. If you do not wish them to be worn this way, make the sleeves 1½" [3.8cm] shorter.

Instructions

Back
With larger needles, use the long-tail cast-on method to cast on 92 (102, 112, 122, 132) stitches.

Beginning with a WS row, work in stockinette stitch until piece measures 2" [5cm] from cast-on edge, ending after working a RS row.

Next row (WS): P30 (35, 40, 45, 50), place marker, p32, place marker, p30 (35, 40, 45, 50).

Decrease row (RS): K1, skp, knit to 2 stitches before marker, skp, slip marker, k32 (to marker), slip marker, k2tog, knit to last 3 stitches, k2tog, k1.

Work 9 rows even. (Shorten or lengthen the Finished Garment length here, page **12**, by changing the number of rows worked even between decreases.)

Repeat decrease row.

Repeat the last 10 rows twice more—32 stitches between markers, 22 (27, 32, 37, 42) stitches at sides.

Work even for 2" [5cm].

Increase row (RS): K1, increase 1, knit to 1 stitch before marker, increase 1, slip marker, knit to 1 stitch before marker, increase 1, slip marker, knit to last 2 stitches, increase 1, k1.

Work 9 rows even. (Shorten or lengthen the Back Waist length here, page **12**, by changing the number of rows worked even between increases.)

Repeat increase row.

Repeat the last 10 rows twice more—92 (102, 112, 122, 132) stitches.

Work even until the piece measures 14" [35.5cm] from cast-on edge, ending after working a WS row, removing markers on the last row.

Shape Armholes

Next 2 rows: Bind off 4 (5, 7, 9, 11) stitches, work even to end—84 (92, 98, 104, 110) stitches.

Decrease row (RS): K1, skp, knit to last 3 stitches, k2tog, k1.

Purl 1 row.

Repeat the last 2 rows 6 (10, 13, 16, 19) times more—70 stitches. (Adjust the Shoulder width here, page **15**.)

Work even until armhole measures 7½ (8, 8½, 9, 9½)" [19 (20.5, 21.5, 23, 24)cm], ending after working a WS row.

Shape Shoulders

Next 2 rows: Bind off 5 stitches, work even to end—60 stitches.

Shape Right Shoulder and Back Neck

Next row: Bind off 5 stitches, knit to 12 stitches on right needle, place remaining 43 stitches on holder. Turn.

Bind off 1 stitch at the next 2 neck edges and 5 stitches at the next 2 armhole edges.

Shape Left Shoulder and Back Neck

Return to remaining 43 stitches, RS facing. Slip 26 stitches onto a stitch holder.

Knit a RS row over 17 stitches.

At the next armhole edge, bind off 5 stitches.

Bind off 1 stitch at the next 2 neck edges and 5 stitches at the next 2 armhole edges.

Right Front

With larger needles, use the long-tail cast-on method to cast on 45 (50, 55, 60, 65) stitches.

Next row (WS): P30 (35, 40, 45, 50), place marker, p15.

Work even until piece measures 2" [5cm], from cast-on edge, ending after working a RS row.

Decrease row (RS): Knit to marker, k2tog, knit to last 3 stitches, k2tog, k1.

Work 9 rows even. (Shorten or lengthen the Finished Garment length here, page **12**, as for Back.)

Repeat decrease row.

Repeat the last 10 rows twice more—37 (42, 47, 52, 57) stitches.

Work even for 2" [5cm].

Increase row (RS): Knit to marker, increase 1, knit to last 2 stitches, increase 1, k1.

Work 9 rows even. (Shorten or lengthen the Back Waist length here, page **12**, as for Back.)
Repeat increase row.
Repeat the last 10 rows twice more—45 (50, 55, 60, 65) stitches.
Work to same length as Back to armhole, ending after working a RS row and removing marker on the last row.

Shape Armhole
Bind off 4 (5, 7, 9, 11) stitches at the beginning of the next WS row—41 (45, 48, 51, 54) stitches.
Decrease row (RS): Knit to last 3 stitches, k2tog, k1.
Purl 1 row.
Repeat the last 2 rows 7 (11, 14, 17, 20) times more—33 stitches. (Adjust the Shoulder width here, page **15**, as for Back.)
Work even until armhole measures 5½ (6, 6½, 7, 7½)" [14 (15, 16.5, 18, 19)cm] from cast-on edge, ending after working a WS row.

Shape Neck
Bind off 4 stitches at the next neck edge, 3 stitches at the next neck edge, 2 stitches at the next neck edge, then 1 stitch at the next 4 neck edges—20 stitches.
Work even until armholes measures same length as Back, ending after working a RS row.

Shape Shoulder
Bind off 5 stitches at the next 4 armhole edges.

Left Front
Work as for Right Front until piece measures 2" [5cm] from cast-on edge, ending after working a RS row.
Next row (WS): P15, place marker, p30 (35, 40, 45, 50).
Decrease row (RS): K1, skp, knit to 2 stitches before marker, skp, slip marker, knit to end.
Work 9 rows even. (Shorten or lengthen the Finished Garment length here, page **12**, as for Back.)
Repeat decrease row.
Repeat the last 10 rows twice more—37 (42, 47, 52, 57) stitches.
Work even for 2" [5cm].
Increase row (RS): K1, increase 1, knit to stitch before marker, increase 1, slip marker, knit to end.

Work 9 rows even. (Shorten or lengthen the Back Waist length here, page **12**, as for Back.)
Repeat increase row.
Repeat the last 10 rows twice more—45 (50, 55, 60, 65) stitches.
Work even to same length as Back to armhole, ending after working a WS row and removing marker on the last row.

Shape Armhole
Bind off 4 (5, 7, 9, 11) stitches at the beginning of the next row—41 (45, 48, 51, 54) stitches.
Purl 1 row.
Decrease row (RS): K1, skp, knit to end.
Purl 1 row.
Repeat the last 2 rows 7 (11, 14, 17, 20) times more—33 stitches. (Adjust the Shoulder width here, page **15**, as for Back.)
Work even until piece measures 5½ (6, 6½, 7, 7½)" [14 (15, 16.5, 18, 19)cm] above armhole, ending after working a RS row.

Shape Neck and Shoulder
Work as for Right Front, Shape Neck and Shape Shoulder.

Sleeve (Make 2)
With larger needles and the long-tail cast-on method, cast on 38 (42, 46, 50, 54) stitches. Beginning with a WS row, work in stockinette stitch for 7 rows.
Increase row (RS): K1, increase 1, knit to last 2 stitches, increase 1, k1.
Work 5 (5, 5, 3, 3) rows even.
Repeat the last 6 (6, 6, 4, 4) rows 15 (16, 18, 20, 22) times more—70 (76, 84, 92, 100) stitches.
Work even until piece measures 16" [40.5cm] from cast-on edge, ending after working a WS row. (Shorten or lengthen the Sleeve length here, page **13**.)

Shape Cap
Next 2 rows: Bind off 4 (5, 7, 9, 11) stitches, work in pattern as established—62 (66, 70, 74, 78) stitches.
Decrease row (RS): K1, skp, knit to last 3 stitches, k2tog, k1.
Purl 1 row.
Repeat the last 2 rows 15 (17, 19, 21, 23) times more—30 stitches.

Next 2 rows: Bind off 2 stitches, work even to end—26 stitches.
Next 2 rows: Bind off 4 stitches, work even to end—18 stitches.
Bind off all remaining stitches.

Finishing
Steam-press all pieces.

Left Front Button Band
Row 1 (pick-up row): With RS facing and larger needles, pick up and knit 3 stitches for every 5 rows. (**Note:** To work 3 stitches for 5 rows, pick up and knit 1 stitch in 2 rows then pick up and knit 2 stitches in 3 rows.)
Row 2 (WS): Purl.
Row 3 (RS): Knit.
Rows 4-7: Repeat Rows 2 and 3 twice to work in stockinette stitch.
Row 8 (turn row) (WS): Knit.
Row 9 (RS): Knit.
Rows 10-14: Work even in stockinette, beginning with a purl row.
Bind off loosely and cut the yarn, leaving a long tail.
Using the long tail and a yarn needle, sew bind-off row to selvedge. Sew lower edge of band closed.
Steam-press band.
Mark spaces for 7 evenly spaced buttons, with the first 1" [2.5cm] from the top and the last 4" [10cm] from the bottom.

Right Front Buttonhole Band
Work as for Left Front Button Band to end of Row 3.
Make buttonholes to match placement of buttons as follows.
Row 4 (WS): Make buttonholes while purling the row, [yo, p2tog] at all marked spaces—7 buttonholes made.
Rows 5-7: Work even in stockinette stitch, beginning with a knit row.
Row 8 (turn row) (WS): Knit.
Row 9 (RS): Knit.
Rows 10 and 11: Work even in stockinette, beginning with a purl row.
Row 12 (WS): Make buttonholes, in same manner and in same place as for Row 4, on WS of band.
Rows 13-14: Work even in stockinette.
Bind off loosely, leaving a long tail.
With long tail, sew bind-off row to selvedge, and sew buttonholes together. Sew lower edge of band closed.
Steam-press band.

Neck Band
Sew shoulder seams.
With RS facing and smaller needles, begin at upper edge of Right Front band to pick up and knit as follows:
2 stitches for every 3 rows through both layers at top edge of Front bands,
1 stitch for every bind-off stitch and 1 stitch for every 2-row step between bind-off stitches around Front and Back neck shaping,
1 stitch for every stitch on holder,
3 stitches for every 4 rows along rows worked even—96 stitches.
(Count stitches. If needed, adjust decreases on next row.)
Row 2 (WS): [P8, p2tog] 3 times, [p4, p2tog] 6 times, [p8, p2tog] twice, purl to end—85 stitches.
Rows 3-4: Work even in stockinette.
Row 5 (RS): Make buttonhole as follows: k3, yo, k2tog, knit to end.
Row 6: Purl.
Rows 7-9: Knit.
Row 10: Purl.
Row 11 (RS): Make buttonhole, in same manner and in same place, as Row 5 to make buttonhole on WS of band.
Rows 12-13: Work even in stockinette.
Row 14 (WS): [P8, increase in next stitch] 3 times, [p4, increase in next stitch] 6 times, [p8, increase in next stitch] twice, purl to end—96 stitches.
With larger needle, bind off loosely, leaving a long tail.
With long tail and yarn needle, sew bind-off row to selvedge, and sew buttonhole together.
Sew open edges of band closed.
Steam-press band.
Sew buttons onto Left Front band to correspond to buttonholes on Right Front band.

Collar
With RS facing and smaller needles, begin in 4th stitch from edge of Right Front neck band. Pick up and knit 9 stitches for every 10 purl bumps along edge of neck band, ending in 4th stitch from edge of Left Front neck band—73 stitches.
Next row (WS): Cast on 1 stitch at the beginning of row, purl across. Turn. Cast on 1 stitch—75 stitches.
Increase row (RS): K2, increase 1, knit to last 3 stitches, increase 1, k2.
Work 3 rows even.

Repeat the last 4 rows 4 times more—85 stitches. (Lengthen collar here, if desired, by making more rows, increasing each alternate RS row, as above.)
Purl 1 row.
Knit 1 row.
Change to larger needles.
Turn row (WS): Knit.
Next 2 rows: Work even in stockinette, beginning with a knit row.
Decrease row (RS): K2, skp, knit to last 4 stitches, k2tog, k2.
Work 3 rows even.
Repeat the last 4 rows 4 times more—75 stitches.
Purl 1 row.
Last row (RS): Bind off 1 stitch, knit to end. Turn. P1, slip 1, bind off 1 stitch, slip 1 stitch from the right needle to the left needle. Cut yarn, leaving a 1-yd [0.9m] tail.
Graft live stitches evenly to inside edge of neck band (remembering that there are 9 collar stitches for every 10 stitches of neck band). Pull grafting tight enough to seam but not so tight as to bind.
Taking 1 stitch from each edge into seam allowance, sew open front edges of Collar closed.
Steam-press collar.
Sew Sleeves into armholes.
Sew side and Sleeve seams.

Cuffs

With larger needles, use the long tail cast-on method to cast on 42 (46, 50, 54, 58) stitches. Work even until piece measures 3" [7.5cm] from cast-on edge. End after working a RS row.

Turn row (WS): Knit.
Work even until piece measures 3" [7.5cm] past turn row, ending after working a WS row.
Last row (RS): Bind off 1 stitch, knit to end. Turn. P1, slip 1, bind off 1 stitch, slip 1 stitch from the right needle to the left needle. Cut yarn, leaving a 1-yd [0.9m] tail.
With RS facing, graft live stitches to cast-on edge of Sleeve as follows:

Attach Right Cuff
Hold cuff above Sleeve, matching 1st stitch of cuff to 8th stitch to left of Sleeve seam.
*Beginning at this point, and grafting from right to left, graft stitches of cuff to cast-on row of Sleeve—4 stitches.
Sew remaining 4 stitches to cast-on row under grafted edge of cuff.

Attach Left Cuff
Hold cuff below Sleeve, matching 1st stitch of cuff to 8th stitch to left of Sleeve seam.
Work as for Attach Right Cuff from * to end.

Both Cuffs
Fold cuffs over, and steam-press.
Sew cast-on edges of cuffs to seam allowances.
Taking 1 stitch from each edge into seam allowance, sew open edges of cuffs closed.
Sew 1 button through all layers of each cuff. To wear cuffs turned back, sew a button to WS of each cuff.

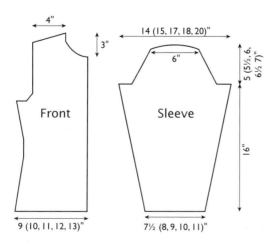

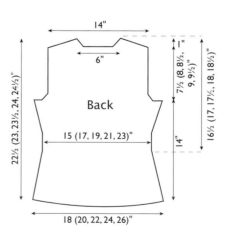

SPRINGTIME IN PARIS SHRUG

by Berta Karapetyan

Beat those winter-weekend blahs with this jaunty wool–cashmere shrug. Careful construction and shaping create the tapered sleeves, raglan armholes, and a brioche ribbing pattern that make this piece a wardrobe classic.

Intermediate

Sizes
S (M, L, XL)

Finished Measurements
Bust: 34 (36, 38, 40)" [86 (91.5, 96.5, 101.5)cm]
Length: 18 (18½, 19, 19½)" [46 (47, 48, 49.5)cm]
Upper arm: 11 (12, 13, 14)" [28 (30.5, 33, 35.5) cm]

Materials
1386 (1386, 1540, 1694) yd [1260 (1260, 1400, 1540)m] / 9 (9, 10, 11) balls Karabella Margrite (80% extra fine merino wool, 20% cashmere, each approximately 1¾ oz [50g] and 154 yd [140m]), in color #9096 Spring Green, (3) light/ DK weight
1 Pair size 11 [8mm] needles, or size needed to obtain gauge

1 Pair size 5 [3.75mm] needles, or size needed to obtain gauge
Stitch markers
Yarn needle

Gauge
12 stitches and 14 rows = 4" [10cm] over Brioche Stitch using 2 strands of yarn held together on size 11 [8mm] needles
24 stitches and 30 rows = 4" [10cm] over stockinette stitch using size 5 [3.75mm] needles

Pattern Stitch
Brioche Stitch (over an even number of stitches)
Set-up row: Slip 1, *yo, slip 1, k1; repeat from * to 1 stitch before end of row, k1.
Row 1: Sllp 1, *yo, slip 1, k2tog (slip stitch and yo of previous row); repeat from *, k1.
Repeat Row 1 for Brioche Stitch.

Instructions

Body
With larger needles and 2 strands of yarn held together, cast on 46 stitches.
Work even in Brioche Stitch until piece measures 44 (46, 48, 50)" [112 (117, 122, 127)cm] from cast-on edge.
Bind off all stitches.
Fold the piece in half, and place marker at fold to indicate center back. Place 2 additional markers 9 (9½, 10, 10½)" [23 (24, 25, 26.5)cm] on either side of the center back.
With RS facing, starting from right marker, with smaller needles and a single strand of yarn, pick up and knit 108 (114, 120, 126) stitches evenly spaced between the rightmost and leftmost markers, ending at left marker.

Shape Back
Row 1 (RS): K1, k2tog, knit to last 3 stitches, ssk, k1—106 (112, 118, 124) stitches.
Row 2 and all WS rows: Purl.

Size S Only
Repeat these 2 rows 21 times—66 stitches (42 rows total).

Size M Only
Repeat these 2 rows 23 times, omitting decreases on Rows 9 and 29—72 stitches remain (46 rows total).

Size L Only
Repeat these 2 rows 25 times, omitting decreases on Rows 9, 19, 29, and 39—78 stitches remain (50 rows total).

Size XL Only
Repeat these 2 rows 27 times, omitting decreases on Rows 9, 19, 29, 39, and 49—84 stitches remain (54 rows total).

For All Sizes
Bind off all stitches.

Sleeve (Make 2)

With smaller needles and a single strand of yarn, cast on 46 (48, 50, 52) stitches.

Rows 1-4: *K1, p1; repeat from * to end.

Work even in stockinette stitch for 10 rows.

Increase row (RS): K1, M1, knit to last stitch, M1, k1—48 (50, 52, 54) stitches.

Repeat this increase row every 12 (10, 9, 8) rows 9 (11, 13, 15) times more—66 (72, 78, 84) stitches.

Work even until piece measures 17½" [44.5cm] from cast-on edge.

Shape Cap

Row 1 (RS): K1, k2tog, knit to last 3 stitches, ssk, k1—64 (70, 76, 82) stitches.

Row 2 (WS): P1, ssp, purl to last 3 stitches, p2tog, p1—62 (68, 74, 80) stitches.

Work these decreases on every row until 2 stitches remain—42 (46, 50, 54) rows, omitting decreases on rows 4, 8, 12, 16, 20, 24, 28,

32, 36, and 40 for all sizes. Additionally, omit decreases on Row 44 for sizes M, L, and XL, and on Row 48 for L and XL, and on Row 52 for XL only.

Work last 2 stitches as ssk on RS row.

Fasten off remaining stitch.

Finishing

Using a yarn needle, sew backs of the Sleeves to the upper Back (knitted with 1 strand of yarn). Match the two ends (cast-on and bind-off edges) of Body with the center of upper back. Starting from center of upper back, sew half of the Body to upper back, then down the fronts of the Sleeves. Return to center of upper back, and working in the opposite direction from the 1st half, sew 2nd half of Body to upper back and fronts of Sleeves. Starting from the center upper back, sew 2½" [6.5cm] of the Body together along the cast-on and bind-off edges to form the collar.

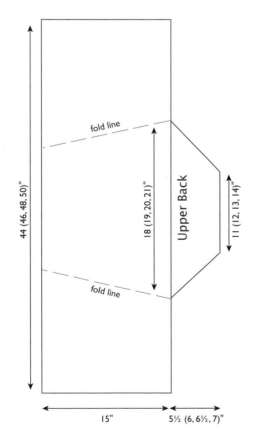

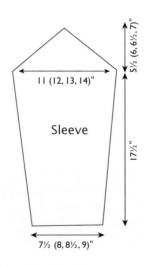

SOPHISTICATED HOODIE

by Sally Melville

A hoodie doesn't have to be shapeless! This piece is meant to be comfy with its all-season yarn and not-too-tight fit. But it's also a great example of how shaping can change a slouchy piece into a slimming one. What's more, it is worked in a reversible stitch pattern so the inside of the hood will look as nice as the outside.

Skill Level
Experienced

Sizes
S (M, L, 1X, 2X)

Finished Measurements
Bust: 37½ (42, 45½, 50, 53½)" [95 (106.5, 115.5, 127, 136)cm]
Hem: 40 (45, 48, 53, 56)" [101.5 (114.5, 122, 134.5, 139.5)cm]
Length: 22 (22½, 23, 23½, 24)" [56 (57, 58.5, 59.5, 61)cm]
Shoulder width: 15" [38cm]
Waist length: 15½ (16, 16½, 17, 17½)" [39 (40.5, 42, 43, 44.5)cm]
Sleeve length: 29 (29½, 30, 30½, 31)" [73.5 (75, 76, 77.5, 78.5)cm]

Materials
1575 (1750, 1925, 2100, 2275) yd [1420 (1575, 1735, 1890, 2050)m] / 9 (10, 11, 12, 13) balls Rowan Calmer (75% cotton, 25% acrylic/microfiber, each approximately 1¾ oz [50g] and 175 yd [160m]), in color #492 Garnet, (3) light/DK weight
1 Pair size 6 [4mm] needles, or size needed to obtain gauge
1 Pair size 4 [3.5mm] needles
1 Pair size 8 [5mm] needles
Stitch markers
Stitch holder
Yarn needle
Separating zipper, 18" [45cm] long
Sewing thread (optional)

Gauge
22 stitches and 32 rows – 4" [10cm)] over stockinette or stitch pattern using size 6 [4mm] needles (after blocking)

Pattern Notes
This garment is hourglass shaped so it could fall between your ideal lengths for Short and Midlength Sweaters.
This garment also is high-waisted. You may adjust Back Waist length (between the waist and armhole) and Finished Garment length (between the waist and hem) as indicated on page 12.
While the Squares Stitch pattern is reversible, the pattern demands a designation of right- and wrong-side rows.
The second section of the Squares Stitch pattern starts on a wrong-side row.
Maintain all stitch patterns as established through the shaping and work-even directions. Work all increases as lifted increases—knitwise in a knit stitch, purlwise in a purl stitch.

Stitch Pattern
Squares Stitch Pattern (over a multiple of 10 stitches)
Rows 1, 3, 5, and 7 (RS): *P1, [k1, p1] twice, k5; repeat from * to end.
Row 2, 4, and 6 (WS): *P5, [p1, k1] twice, p1; repeat from * to end.
Rows 8, 10, 12, and 14 (WS): *K1, [p1, k1] twice, k5; repeat from * to end.
Rows 9, 11, and 13 (RS): *P5, [p1, k1] twice, p1; repeat from * to end.
(See Chart, page 97.)

Instructions

Back

Edging

With middle-size needles, use the long-tail cast-on method to cast on 106 (118, 128, 140, 150) stitches.
Purl 1 row.
Knit 1 row.
Purl 2 rows.

Body

Row 1 (RS): K2, p19 (25, 30, 36, 41), k2, place marker, work 10-stitch repeat of Squares Stitch pattern over next 60 stitches, place marker, k2, purl to last 2 stitches, k2.
Row 2 (WS): P2, k19 (25, 30, 36, 41), p2, work 10-stitch repeat of Squares Stitch pattern over next 60 stitches, p2, knit to last 2 stitches, p2.
Repeat Rows 1 and 2 five times more, ending after working a WS row—12 rows, total.
Decrease row (RS): K1, skp, purl to 3 stitches before marker, k2tog, k1, slip marker, work 10-stitch repeat over next 60 stitches, k1, skp, purl to last 3 stitches, k2tog, k1—102 (114, 124, 136, 146) stitches.
Work 11 rows even. (Shorten or lengthen the Finished Garment length here, page **12**, by changing number of rows worked even between decreases.)
Repeat decrease row.
Repeat the last 12 rows twice more—90 (102, 112, 124, 134) stitches. (Piece measures 6½" [16.5cm] from cast-on edge).
Work even for 3" [7.5cm].
Increase row (RS): K2, increase 1, purl to 2 stitches before marker, k2, slip marker, work 10-stitch repeat over next 60 stitches, k2, purl to last 3 stitches, increase 1, k2—92 (104, 114, 126, 136) stitches.
Work 5 rows even.
Repeat increase row.
Repeat the last 6 rows 3 times more—100 (112, 122, 134, 144) stitches.
Work even until piece measures 13½" [34cm], ending after working a WS row. (Shorten or lengthen the Back Waist length here, page **12**.)

Shape Armholes

Next 2 rows: Bind off 4 (5, 7, 9, 12) stitches, work in pattern as established—92 (102, 108, 116, 120) stitches.
Decrease row (RS): K1, skp, purl to 2 stitches before marker, k2, slip marker, work 10-stitch repeat over next 60 stitches, k2, purl to last 3 stitches, k2tog, k1.
Work next WS row.
*Repeat decrease row.
Work next WS row.
Decrease row with princess shaping (RS): K1, skp, purl to 3 stitches before marker, k2tog, k1, slip marker, increase 1, work Squares Stitch pattern to 1 stitch before marker, increase 1, slip marker, k1, skp, purl to last 3 stitches, k2tog, k1.
Work next WS row.
Repeat from * until 84 stitches remain. (Adjust Shoulder width here, page **12**.)
Princess shaping (RS): Work as established to 3 stitches before marker, k2tog, k1, slip marker, increase 1, work Squares Stitch pattern to stitch before marker, increase 1, slip marker, k1, skp, work as established.
Repeat princess shaping row at the beginning and end of every other RS row until k4 stitches remain.
Repeat princess shaping row on next 2 RS rows. Remove markers.
Following WS rows: P2, work 10-stitch repeat over next 80 stitches, p2.
Following RS rows: K2, work 10-stitch repeat over next 80 stitches, k2.
Work even until armhole measures 4½ (5, 5½, 6, 6½)" [11.5 (12.5, 14, 15, 16.5)cm], ending after working a WS row.
(**Note:** The stitch pattern will look best if you end after Row 8 or 14, but it is not essential.)

Shape Shoulders

Next 6 rows: Bind off 6 stitches, work in pattern as established—48 stitches.
Next 2 rows: Bind off 7 stitches, work in pattern as established—34 stitches.
Bind off all remaining stitches.

10-stitch repeat over next 30 stitches, k3—54 (60, 65, 71, 76) stitches.

Work 11 rows even.

Repeat decrease row.

Repeat the last 12 rows twice more—48 (54, 59, 65, 70) stitches. (Piece measures 6½" [16.5cm] from cast-on edge).

Work even for 3" [7.5cm].

Increase row (RS): K2, increase 1, purl to 2 stitches before marker, k2, slip marker, work 10-stitch repeat over next 30 stitches, k3.

Work 5 rows even.

Repeat increase row.

Repeat the last 6 rows 3 times more—53 (59, 64, 70, 75) stitches.

Work even until piece measures same length as Back to armhole, ending after working a WS row.

Shape Armhole

Next row: Bind off 4 (5, 7, 9, 12) stitches, work in pattern as established—49 (54, 57, 61, 63) stitches.

Decrease row (RS): K1, skp, purl to 2 stitches before marker, k2, slip marker, work 10-stitch repeat over next 30 stitches, k3.

Work next WS row.

*Repeat decrease row.

Work next WS row.

Decrease row with princess shaping (RS): K1, skp, purl to 3 stitches before marker, k2tog, k1, slip marker, increase 1, work squares stitch pattern to last 3 stitches, k3.

Work next WS row.

Repeat from * until 45 stitches remain. (Adjust shoulder width here, page **15**, as for Back.)

Princess shaping (RS): Work in pattern as established to 3 stitches before marker, k2tog, k1, slip marker, increase 1, work Squares Stitch pattern to last 3 stitches, k3.

Repeat princess shaping row every alternate RS row until k4 remains at the beginning and at the end of RS rows beginning of a RS row.

Repeat princess shaping row next 2 RS rows, removing marker while working the last row.

Subsequent WS rows: P3, work 10-stitch repeat over next 40 stitches, p2.

Subsequent RS rows: K2, work 10-stitch repeat over next 40 stitches, k3.

Work even until armhole measures same length as Back, ending after working a WS row.

Left Front

Edging

With middle-size needles, use the long-tail cast-on method to cast on 56 (62, 67, 73, 78) stitches.

Purl 1 row.

Knit 1 row.

Purl 2 rows.

Body

Row 1 (RS): K2, p19 (25, 30, 36, 41), k2, place marker, work 10-stitch repeat of Squares Stitch pattern over next 30 stitches, k3.

Row 2 (WS): P3, work 10-stitch repeat of Squares Stitch pattern over next 30 stitches, p2, knit to last 2 stitches, p2.

Repeat Rows 1 and 2 five times more, ending after working a WS row—12 rows, total. (Shorten or lengthen the Finished Garment length here, page **12**, as for Back.)

Decrease row (RS): K1, skp, purl to 3 stitches before marker, k2tog, k1, slip marker, work

Body

Row 1 (RS): K3, work 10-stitch repeat of Squares Stitch pattern over next 30 stitches, k2, p19 (25, 30, 36, 41), k2.

Row 2 (WS): P2, k19 (25, 30, 36, 41), p2, work 10-stitch repeat of Squares Stitch pattern over next 30 stitches, p3.

Repeat Rows 1 and 2 five times more, ending after working a WS row—12 rows, total. (Shorten or lengthen the Back Waist length here, page **12,** as for Back.)

Decrease row (RS): K3, work 10-stitch repeat over next 30 stitches, k1, skp, purl to last 3 stitches, k2tog, k1—54 (60, 65, 71, 76) stitches.

Work 11 rows even.

Repeat decrease row.

Repeat the last 12 rows twice more—48 (54, 59, 65, 70) stitches. (Piece measures 6½" [16.5cm] from cast-on edge).

Work even for 3" [7.5cm].

Increase row (RS): K3, work 10-stitch repeat over next 30 stitches, k2, purl to last 3 stitches, increase 1, k2.

Work 5 rows even.

Repeat increase row.

Repeat the last 6 rows 3 times more—53 (59, 64, 70, 75) stitches.

Work even until piece measures same length as Back to armhole, ending after working a RS row.

Shape Armhole

Bind off 4 (5, 7, 9, 12) stitches at the beginning of the next row—49 (54, 57, 61, 63) stitches.

Decrease row (RS): K3, work 10-stitch repeat over next 30 stitches, place marker, k2, purl to last 3 stitches, k2tog, k1.

Work next WS row.

*Repeat decrease row.

Work next WS row.

Decrease row with princess shaping (RS): K3, work Squares Stitch pattern to 1 stitch before marker, increase 1, slip marker, k1, skp, purl to last 3 stitches, k2tog, k1.

Work next WS row.

Repeat from * until 45 stitches remain. (Adjust Shoulder width here, page **15,** as for Back.)

Princess shaping (RS): K3, work Squares Stitch pattern to 1 stitch before marker, increase 1, slip marker, k1, skp, work in pattern as established.

Repeat princess shaping row every alternate RS row until k4 remains at end of RS row.

Shape Shoulder

Bind off 6 stitches at the next 3 armhole edges, and 7 stitches at the next armhole edge—20 stitches.

Bind off all remaining stitches.

Right Front

Edging

With middle-size needles, use the long-tail cast-on method to cast on 56 (62, 67, 73, 78) stitches.

Purl 1 row.

Knit 1 row.

Purl 2 rows.

Repeat princess shaping row next 2 RS rows. Remove marker.

Subsequent WS rows: P2, work 10-stitch repeat over next 40 stitches, p3.

Subsequent RS rows: K3, work 10-stitch repeat over next 40 stitches, k2.

Work even until armhole measures same length as Back, ending after working a RS row.

Shape Shoulder

Work as for Left Front, Shape Shoulder.

Right Sleeve

Edging

With middle-size needles, use the long-tail cast-on method to cast on 40 (40, 46, 46, 54) stitches.
Purl 1 row.
Knit 1 row.
Purl 2 rows.

Body

Beginning with a knit row, work stockinette stitch until piece measures 1" [2.5cm] from cast-on edge, ending after working a WS row.

Increase row (RS): K2, increase 1, knit to last 3 stitches, increase 1, k2.

Work even in stockinette stitch for 5 (5, 5, 3, 3) rows more.

Repeat the last 6 (6, 6, 4, 4) rows 16 (19, 20, 24, 26) times more—74 (80, 88, 96, 108) stitches.

Work even until piece measures 17" [43cm] from cast-on edge, ending after working a WS row. (Shorten or lengthen the Sleeve length here, page **13**.)

Shape Cap

Next 2 rows: Bind off 4 (5, 7, 9, 12) stitches, work in pattern as established—66 (70, 74, 78, 84) stitches.

Decrease row (RS): K1, skp, knit to last 3 stitches, k2tog, k1.

Work next WS row.

Repeat the last 2 rows 16 (18, 20, 22, 25) times more—32 stitches.

Sleeve Saddle

Work even for 4" [10cm], ending after working a WS row.

Shape Front Neck

Next row (short row) (RS) K16. Turn. At Front neck edge, bind off 5 stitches once, 3 stitches once, 2 stitches once, then 1 stitch until 2 stitches remain.
Bind off all stitches.

Shape Back Neck

On the remaining 16 stitches and with RS facing, work rows at the Back neck edge as follows:

Next row: Bind off 2 stitches, work in pattern as established.

Next 2 rows: Bind off 1 stitch, work in pattern as established—12 stitches.

Work even over 12 stitches until neck opening measures 3½" [9cm]. Slip stitches to a stitch holder.

Left Sleeve

Work as for Right Sleeve to Sleeve Saddle.

Sleeve Saddle

Work even for 4" [10cm], ending after working a RS row.

Shape Front Neck

Next row (short row) (WS): P16. Turn. Work rows at the Front neck edge, binding off 5 stitches at the beginning of each row once, 3 stitches once, 2 stitches once, then 1 stitch until 2 stitches remain.
Bind off all stitches.

Shape Back Neck

On the remaining 16 stitches and with WS facing, work rows at the Back neck edge as follows:

Next row: Bind off 2 stitches, work in pattern as established.

Next 2 rows: Bind off 1 stitch, work in pattern as established—12 stitches.

Work even over 12 stitches until neck opening measures 3½" [9cm]. Slip stitches to a stitch holder.

Finishing

Using a yarn needle, sew long edges of Sleeve saddles to top of Back. (**Note:** You may need to add or delete rows so the saddles meet at the center.)

Using a yarn needle, graft or sew live stitches together.

Sew front edges of Sleeve saddles to tops of Fronts, ending approximately 2" [5cm] from Front edges.

Neck Edging

With RS facing and smallest needles, beginning at Right Front neck, pick up and knit 12 stitches along tops of Fronts, 25 stitches around Front and Back neck shaping, and 35 stitches along straight edge of Back neck—109 stitches.
Knit 1 row (WS).
Purl 1 row.
Knit 1 row.
Purl 2 rows.
Increase row (RS): K2, *increase 1, k3; repeat from * to last 3 stitches, increase 1, k2—136 stitches.
At any time while knitting the Hood, sew this last row to the pick-up row of the neck edging.

Hood

Change to middle-size needles.
Next row (WS): P3, beginning with Row 8, work 10-stitch repeat of Squares Stitch pattern to last 3 stitches, p3.
RS rows: K3, work 10-stitch repeat of squares to last 3 stitches, k3.
WS rows: P3, work 10-stitch repeat of Squares Stitch pattern to last 3 stitches, p3.
Repeat these last 2 rows until the Hood measures approximately 12" [30.5cm] from the pick-up row, ending after working Row 8 or 14.
Next row (short row) (RS): K3, work 65 stitches (to center of Hood). Turn. Work over this side of Hood only as follows:
WS row: Bind off 8 stitches, work in pattern as established.
RS row: Work in pattern as established.
Repeat the last 2 rows twice more—44 stitches.
Slip these stitches to a stitch holder.
RS row: On the remaining 68 stitches, with RS facing, bind off 8 stitches, work in pattern as established.
WS row: Work next WS row in pattern as established.
Repeat the last 2 rows twice more—44 stitches.
Turn the Hood to WS and work 3-needle bind-off over 44 stitches of each side.
Turn the Hood to the right side, and sew the bound-off edges together.

Front and Hood Edging

With RS facing and smallest needles, and beginning at lower Right Front edge, pick up and knit 2 stitches for every 3 rows up Right Front, around Hood, and down Left Front.

Knit 1 row.
Purl 1 row.
Knit 1 row.
Bind off purlwise and cut yarn, leaving a long tail. With long tail and a yarn needle, sew bind-off row of edging to selvedge. (**Note:** The edging may seem like it has too few stitches, but the zipper will stretch it straight.)

Zipper

Baste the zipper into the WS of the Fronts (so the teeth end at edge of the edging).
Cut the tab at the top of the zipper as needed so it doesn't extend into the Hood.
With thinned project yarn (or matching sewing thread), use a backstitch to sew in the zipper.

Right Front Zipper Facing

Turn Right Front to WS.
Find the purl stitch at the edge of the zipper (the stitch before the Squares Stitch pattern).
Beginning at the top of the zipper, slip largest needle through the purl bumps of this stitch, every 2nd row, along the length of the zipper.
*Knit 1 row (WS).
Purl 1 row.
Knit 1 row.
Bind off purlwise and very loosely. Cut yarn, leaving a long tail.
With the long tail, blind hem the zipper facing to the zipper, hiding all stitching (but not so it will interfere the with the movement of the zipper).

Left Front Zipper Facing

Find the purl stitch at the edge of the zipper (the stitch before the Squares Stitch pattern).
Beginning at the bottom of the zipper, slip the largest needle through the purl bumps of this stitch, every 2nd row, along the length of the zipper.
Work as for Right Front Zipper Facing from * to end.
Using Yarn needle and project yarn, sew Sleeves into armholes. Sew side and Sleeve seams.

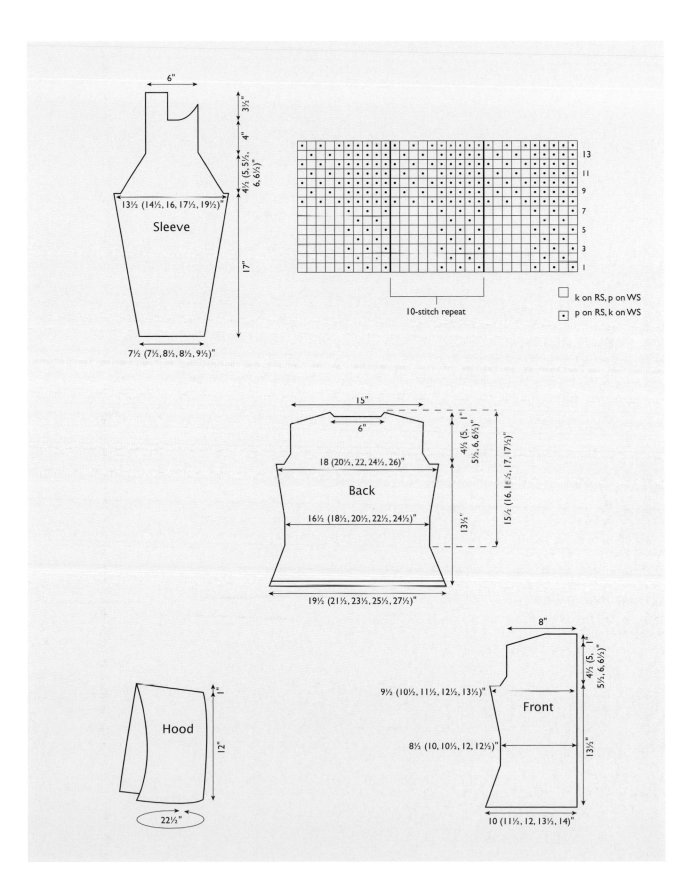

6"

3½"

4"

4½ (5, 5½, 6, 6½)"

13½ (14½, 16, 17½, 19½)"

Sleeve

17"

7½ (7½, 8½, 8½, 9½)"

13

11

9

7

5

3

1

10-stitch repeat

☐ k on RS, p on WS

⊡ p on RS, k on WS

15"

1"

6"

4½ (5, 5½, 6, 6½)"

18 (20½, 22, 24½, 26)"

Back

15½ (16, 16½, 17, 17½)"

16½ (18½, 20½, 22½, 24½)"

13½"

19½ (21½, 23½, 25½, 27½)"

1"

Hood

12"

22½"

8"

4½ (5, 5½, 6, 6½)"

1"

9½ (10½, 11½, 12½, 13½)"

Front

8½ (10, 10½, 12, 12½)"

13½"

10 (11½, 12, 13½, 14)"

RUFFLED CARDIGAN

by Berta Karapetyan

This piece's set-in armhole, shoulder shaping, and semifitted waist make it a close-fitting garment when closed. Knitting it will help you learn to create perfectly laid ruffles—in this case, down the front and at the sleeves. This graceful, feminine cardigan is fun to wear and has just a hint of attitude.

Skill Level
Experienced

Sizes
S (M, l)

Finished Measurements
Bust: 32 (36, 40)" [81 (91.5, 101.5)cm]
Length (with ruffle): 23 (23½, 24)" [58.5 (60, 61)cm]
Upper arm: 11 (12, 13)" [28 (30.5, 33)cm]
Sleeve length (with ruffle): 24 (24½, 25)" [61 (62, 63.5)cm]

Materials
1372 (1568, 1764) yd [1260 (1440, 1620)m] / 7 (8, 9) balls Karabella Aurora 4 (100% extra fine merino wool, each approximately 1¾ oz [50g] and 196 yd [180m]), in color #1148 Black, (2) fine/sport weight
1080 yd [1000m] / 2 balls Karabella Lace Mohair (61% super kid mohair, 8% wool, 31% polyester, each approximately 1¾ oz [50g] and 540 yd [500m]), in color #250, Black, (1) super fine/lace weight
1 Pair size 2 [2.75mm] needles, or size needed to obtain gauge
1 Size 7 [4.5mm] circular needle, 24" [60cm] long, or size needed to obtain gauge
Yarn needle

Gauge
30 stitches and 40 rows = 4" [10cm] over stockinette stitch using size 2 [2.75mm] needles and Aurora 4
20 stitches and 30 rows = 4" [10cm] over stockinette stitch using size 7 [4.5mm] needle and Lace Mohair

Pattern Stitches
Wide Ruffle (over 28 stitches)
Row 1 (RS): Knit to last 4 stitches, wrap the next stitch, and turn work, leaving remaining stitches unworked.
Row 2 and all WS rows to Row 16: Slip wrapped stitch, work stitches as they appear to end of row.
Row 3: Knit to last 7 stitches, wrap next stitch, turn work.
Row 5: Knit to last 10 stitches, wrap next stitch, turn work.
Row 7: Knit to last 13 stitches, wrap next stitch, turn work.
Row 9: Knit to last 16 stitches, wrap next stitch, turn work.
Row 11: Knit to last 19 stitches, wrap next stitch, turn work.
Row 13: Knit to last 22 stitches, wrap next stitch, turn work.
Row 15: Knit to last 25 stitches, wrap next stitch, turn work.
Row 17 (smoothing row): K28 while working wraps and knit stitches together when you come to them.
Row 18: P28.
Row 19: K3, wrap next stitch, and turn work, leaving remaining 24 stitches unworked.
Row 20 and all WS rows to Row 34: Slip wrapped stitch, work stitches as they appear to end of row.
Rows 21, 23, 25, 27, 29, 31, and 33: Knit to 1 stitch before wrap, work stitch and its wrap together, k2, wrap next stitch, turn work.
Row 35: Knit to 1 stitch before wrap, work stitch and its wrap together, knit to end—28 stitches.
Row 36: P28.

Narrow Ruffle (over 18 stitches)

Row 1 (RS): Knit to last 3 stitches, wrap next stitch, and turn work, leaving remaining stitch unworked.

Row 2 and all WS rows to Row 10: Slip wrapped stitch, work stitches as they appear to end of row.

Row 3: Knit to last 6 stitches, wrap next stitch, turn work.

Row 5: Knit to last 9 stitches, wrap next stitch, turn work.

Row 7: Knit to last 12 stitches, wrap next stitch, turn work.

Row 9: Knit to last 15 stitches, wrap next stitch, turn work.

Row 11 (smoothing row): K18 while working wrap and knit stitches together when you come to them.

Row 12: P18.

Row 13: K3, wrap next stitch, turn work.

Row 14 and all WS rows to Row 22: Slip wrapped stitch, work stitches as they appear to end.

Rows 15, 17, 19, and 21: Knit to 1 stitch before wrap, work stitch and its wrap together, k2, wrap next stitch, turn work.

Row 23: Knit to 1 stitch before wrap, work stitch and its wrap together, knit to end—18 stitches.

Row 24: P18.

Instructions

Back

With smaller needles and Aurora 4, cast on 120 (136, 152) stitches.

Work even in stockinette stitch for 8 rows.

Decrease row (RS): K2, k2tog, knit to last 4 stitches, ssk, k2—118 (134, 150) stitches.

Repeat decrease row every 8th row 4 times more—110 (126, 142) stitches.

Work even until piece measures 7" [18cm] from cast-on edge, ending after working a WS row.

Increase row (RS): K2, M1, knit to last 2 stitches, M1, k2—112 (128, 144) stitches.

Repeat increase row every 6th row 5 times more—122 (138, 154) stitches.

Work even until piece measures 12" [30.5cm] from cast-on edge, ending after working a WS row.

Shape Armholes

Next 2 rows: Bind off 4 (5, 6) stitches, work in pattern as established—114 (128, 142) stitches.

Decrease row (RS): K2, k2tog, knit to last 4 stitches, ssk, k2—112 (126, 140) stitches.

Repeat decrease row every 4th row 8 (9, 10) times more—96 (108, 120) stitches.

Work even until armhole measures 7½ (8, 8½)" [19 (20.5, 21.5)cm], ending after working a WS row.

Shape Shoulders

Next 2 rows: Bind off 10 (12, 13) stitches, work in pattern as established—76 (84, 94) stitches.

Next 2 rows: Bind off 10 (11, 13) stitches, work in pattern as established—56 (62, 68) stitches.

Next 2 rows: Bind off 10 (11, 12) stitches, work in pattern as established—36 (40, 44) stitches.

Bind off all remaining stitches for Back Neck.

Right Front

With smaller needles and Aurora 4, cast on 20 (28, 36) stitches.

Row 1 (RS) and all RS rows until new instructions are given: Knit.

Rows 2, 4, 6 (WS): Purl to end, cast on 6 stitches—38 (46, 54) stitches after completing Row 6.

Rows 8, 10, 12, 14, 16, 18, 20, and 22 (WS): Purl to end, cast on 2 stitches.

Rows 9, 17, 25, 33, and 41 (decrease): Knit to last 4 stitches, ssk, k2.

Rows 24, 28, 32, 36, 40, and 44: Purl.

Rows 26, 30, 34, 38, 42, and 46: Purl to end, cast on 1 stitch using backward loop method (e-wrap)—55 (63, 71) stitches after completing Row 46.

Work even until piece measures 7" [18cm] from cast-on edge, ending after working a WS row.

Increase row (RS): Knit to last 2 stitches, M1, k2—56 (64, 72) stitches.

Repeat increase row every 6th row 5 times more—61 (69, 77) stitches.

AT THE SAME TIME, when piece measures 10" [25.5cm] from cast-on edge, ending after working a WS row, begin neck shaping as follows.

Shape Neck

Continuing to increase at side edge of Right Front until all increases are completed, shape neck as follows:

Decrease row (RS): K2, k2tog, work to end.

Repeat decrease row every 6th row 11 (9, 7) times more, then every 4th row 6 (10, 14) times—43 (49, 55) stitches.

AT THE SAME TIME, when piece measures approximately 12" [30.5cm] from cast-on edge, after working a RS row, begin armhole shaping.

Shape Armhole

Continuing to decrease at neck edge of Right Front until all increases are completed, shape armhole as follows:

Next row (WS): Bind off 4 (5, 6) stitches, work to end.

Decrease row (RS): Work to last 4 stitches, ssk, k2. Repeat decrease row every 4th row 8 (9, 10) times more.

When neck and armhole shaping has been completed, work even on 30 (34, 38) stitches until armhole measures 7½ (8, 8½)" [19 (20.5, 21.5)cm], ending after working a RS row.

Shape Shoulder

Next row (WS): Bind off 10 (12, 13) stitches, work to end—20 (22, 25) stitches.

Next row (RS): Knit.

Next row (WS): Bind off 10 (11, 13) stitches, work to end—10 (11, 12) stitches.

Next row (RS): Knit.

Bind off all remaining stitches.

Left Front

Using smaller needles and Aurora 4, cast on 20 (28, 36) stitches.

Set-up row: Purl.

Row 1 (RS): Knit to end, cast on 6 stitches—26 (34, 42) stitches.

Row 2 and all WS rows: Purl.

Rows 3 and 5: Knit to end, cast on 6 stitches—38 (46, 54) stitches.

Rows 7, 11, 13, 15, 19, and 21: Knit to end, cast on 2 stitches.

Rows 9 and 17: K2, k2tog, knit to end, cast on 2 stitches.

Rows 23, 27, 31, 35, 39, and 43: Knit.

Rows 25, 33, and 41: K2, k2tog, knit to end, cast on 1 stitch using the e-wrap cast-on.

Rows 29, 37, and 45: Knit to end, cast on 1 stitch using the e-wrap cast-on—55 (63, 71) stitches after Row 45 has been completed.

Work even in stockinette stitch until piece measures 7" [18cm] from cast-on edge, ending after working a WS row.

Increase row (RS): K2, M1, knit to end 56 (64, 72) stitches.

Work in stockinette stitch, repeating this increase row every 6th row 5 times more—61 (69, 77) stitches.

AT THE SAME TIME, when piece measures 10" [25.5cm] from cast-on edge, ending after working a WS row, begin neck shaping as follows

Shape Neck

Continuing to increase at side edge of Left Front until all increases are completed, shape neck as follows:

Decrease row (RS): Knit to last 4 stitches, ssk, k2. Repeat decrease row every 6th row 11 (9, 7) times more, then every 4th row 6 (10, 14) times—43 (49, 55) stitches.

AT THE SAME TIME, when piece measures approximately 12" [30.5cm] from cast-on edge, after working a WS row, begin armhole shaping.

Shape Armhole

Continuing to decrease at neck edge of Left Front until all increases are completed, shape armhole as follows:

Next row (RS): Bind off 4 (5, 6) stitches, work to end.

Next row (WS): Purl.

Decrease row (RS): K2, k2tog, work to end. Repeat decrease row every 4th row 8 (9, 10) times more.

When neck and armhole shaping have been completed, work even on 30 (34, 38) stitches until armhole measures 7½ (8, 8½)" [19 (20.5, 21.5)cm], ending after working a WS row.

Shape Shoulder

Next row (RS): Bind off 10 (12, 13) stitches, work to end—20 (22, 25) stitches.

Next row (WS): Purl.

Next row: Bind off 10 (11, 13) stitches, work to end—10 (11, 12) stitches.

Next row: Purl.

Bind off remaining 10 (11, 12) stitches.

Sleeve (Make 2)

Using smaller needles and Aurora 4, cast on 60 (64, 68) stitches.

Work even in stockinette stitch for 10 rows.

Increase row (RS): K2, M1, knit to last 2 stitches, M1, k2—62 (66, 70) stitches.

Repeat this increase row every 12 (10, 8) rows 10 (12, 14) times more—82 (90, 98) stitches.

Work even until piece measures 13" [33cm] from cast-on edge, ending after working a WS row.

Shape Cap

Next 2 rows: Bind off 5 stitches, work in pattern as established—72 (80, 88) stitches.

Decrease row (RS): K2, k2tog, knit to last 4 stitches, ssk, k2—70 (78, 86) stitches.

Repeat this decrease row every RS row until 20 (22, 24) stitches remain, ending after working a WS row.

Bind off all stitches.

Finishing

Using a yarn needle, sew shoulder seams.

Sew Sleeves into the armholes.

Sew side and Sleeve seams.

Sleeve Ruffle

Using larger needle and Lace Mohair, cast on 28 stitches.

Work in stockinette stitch for 6 (8, 6) rows.

*Next 36 rows: Work Wide Ruffle.

Work even in stockinette stitch for 8 (8, 10) rows.

Repeat from * 3 times more.

Next 36 rows: Work Wide Ruffle.

Work even in stockinette stitch for 6 (8, 6) rows more or until unruffled edge measures 8 (8½, 9)" [20.5 (21.5, 23)cm].

Bind off all stitches.

Using a yarn needle, sew cast-on and bind-off edges of the ruffle together.

Sew the unruffled edge to the bottom of the Sleeve.

Back Ruffle

Using larger needle and Lace Mohair, cast on 18 stitches.

Work in stockinette stitch for 8 rows.

*Next 24 rows: Work Narrow Ruffle.

Work even in stockinette stitch for 10 rows.

Repeat from * 7 (8, 9) times more.

Next 24 rows: Work Narrow Ruffle.

Work even in stockinette stitch for 10 (8, 6) rows or until unruffled edge of the piece measures 16 (18, 20)" [40.5 (46, 51)cm].

Bind off all stitches.

Using a yarn needle, sew the unruffled edge to the bottom of the Back.

Front Ruffle

Measure the length of the edge where you will sew the Front Ruffle as follows: Beginning from the side seam of the Right Front, going along the bottom of the Right Front and up the middle opening of the Right Front, around the neck, down the middle opening of the Left Front, along the bottom of the Left Front to the Left Front seam—approximately 54 (58, 63)" [137 (147.5, 160)cm].

Note: If your measurements are different from above, adjust the number of ruffles (24 rows of 1 Narrow Ruffle, plus 14 rows of stockinette stitch;

piece measures approximately 2½" [6.5cm] along the unruffled edge).

Using larger needle and Lace Mohair, cast on 18 stitches.

Work in stockinette stitch for 14 (12, 12) rows.

*Next 24 rows: Work Narrow Ruffle.

Work even in stockinette stitch for 14 rows.

Repeat from * 20 (22, 24) times more.

Next 24 rows: Work Narrow Ruffle.

Work even in stockinette stitch until unruffled edge of the piece measures approximately 54 (58, 63)" [137, (147.5, 160)cm].

Bind off all stitches.

Using a yarn needle and Lace Mohair, sew the unruffled edge of the Front Ruffle in place, beginning from the side seam of the Right Front, going along the bottom of the Right Front and up the middle opening of the Right Front, around the neck, down the middle opening of the Left Front, along the bottom of the Left Front to the Left Front seam.

Sew side edges of Back Ruffle to side edges of Front Ruffle.

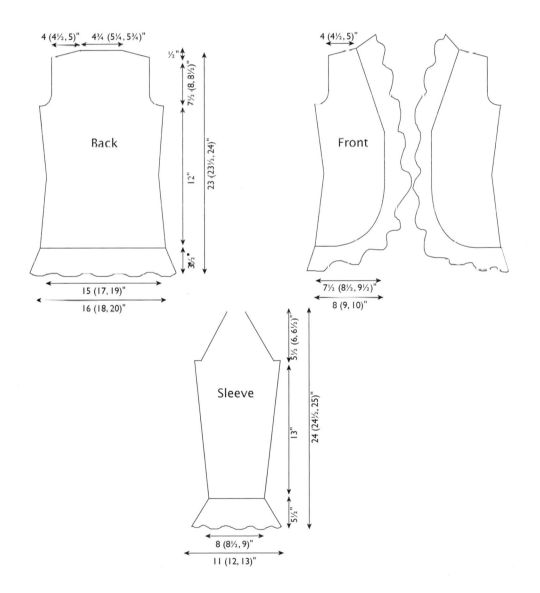

chapter four

SLEEVELESS AND SHORT-SLEEVED TOPS

Knitters don't stop knitting when warmer weather hits. When springtime rolls around, a fitted tank top or short sleeve sweater can show off just the right amount of skin. Mary Weaver's Audrey Pullover is a great transitional piece, with sleeves that cover the upper arm and a neckline that shows off a hint of collarbone. If you dare to bare more, Annie Modesitt's intricate Notorious Low-Cut Top is a challenging option. And when summer ends, many of these tops make great layering pieces for a year-round, hand-knit wardrobe.

SEA FOAM TOP

by Berta Karapetyan

This summery top may be simple to knit, but the little extras—like the hem and eyelet lace—make it truly special. The ruffled V-neck and cap sleeves give it a delicate, playful appeal up top, and the tapered midriff with semifitted waist create a graceful silhouette.

Skill Level
Intermediate

Sizes
S (M, L, XL)

Finished Measurements
Bust: 32 (35, 38, 41)" [81 (89, 96.5, 104)cm]
Length: 22½ (22¾, 23¼, 23½)" [57 (58, 59, 60) cm]

Materials
588 (686, 686, 784) yd (540 [630, 630, 720] m) / 6 (7, 7, 8) balls Karabella Zodiac (100% mercerized cotton, each approximately 1¾ oz [50g] and 98 yd [90m], in color #405 Sea Foam, (4) medium/worsted weight
1 Pair size 4 [3.5mm] needles

1 Size 5 [3.75mm] circular needle, 24" [60cm] long, or size needed to obtain gauge
Yarn needle

Gauge
20 stitches and 30 rows = 4" [10cm] over Easy Eyelet Lace pattern using size 5 [3.75mm] circular needle

Pattern Stitch
Easy Eyelet Lace (over a multiple of 8 stitches)
Row 1 (RS): Knit.
Row 2 and all WS rows: Purl.
Row 3: *K6, yo, k2tog; repeat from * to end.
Row 5: Knit.
Row 7: K2, *yo, k2tog, k6; repeat from * to last 6 stitches, yo, k2tog, k4.
Row 8: Purl.
Repeat Rows 1–8 for Easy Eyelet Lace.

Instructions

Back

With smaller needles, cast on 80 (88, 96, 104) stitches. Work eyelet hem as follows.
Row 1: Knit.
Row 2: Purl.
Row 3 (eyelet hem): K1, *k2tog, yo; repeat from * to last stitch, k1.
Change to larger needles.
Row 4 and all following WS rows: Purl.
Row 5: Knit.
Row 7 (Row 3 of Easy Eyelet Lace): *K6, yo, k2tog; repeat from * to end.
Row 9 (Row 5 of Easy Eyelet Lace): Knit.
Row 11 (Row 7 of Easy Eyelet Lace): K2, *yo, k2tog, k6; repeat from * to last 6 stitches, yo, k2tog, k4.
Row 13 (Row 1 of Easy Eyelet Lace): Knit.
Row 14 (Row 2 of Easy Eyelet Lace): Purl.
Work even in Easy Eyelet Lace until piece measures 2" [5cm] from eyelet hem, ending after working a WS row.

Decrease row (RS): Decrease 1 stitch at the beginning and end of the row (working decreases after the first stitch and before the last stitch)—78 (86, 94, 102) stitches.
Repeat decrease row every 1½" [3.5cm] twice more—74 (82, 90, 98) stitches.
Work even in established pattern for 2" [5cm], ending after working a WS row.
Increase row (RS): Increase 1 stitch at the beginning and end of the next row (work increases after the first stitch and before the last stitch)—76 (84, 92, 100) stitches.
Repeat this increase every 3" [7.5cm] twice more—80 (88, 96, 104) stitches.
Work even in established pattern until piece measures 14½" [37cm] from eyelet hem, ending after working a WS row.

Shape Armholes

Next 2 rows: Bind off 5 (6, 7, 8) stitches, work in pattern as established—70 (76, 82, 88) stitches.

Decrease row (RS): Slip 1, k1, k2tog, work in pattern to last 4 stitches, ssk, k2—68 (74, 80, 86) stitches.

Next row: Slip 1, purl to the end.

Repeat the last 2 rows 4 (5, 6, 7) times more—60 (64, 68, 72) stitches.

Work in pattern as established until armhole measures 7 (7¼, 7¾, 8)" [18 (18.5, 19.5, 20.5)cm].

Shape Shoulders

Next 2 rows: Bind off 5 (5, 5, 6) stitches, work in pattern as established—50 (54, 58, 60) stitches.

Next 2 rows: Bind off 5 (5, 5, 6) stitches, work in pattern as established—40 (44, 48, 48) stitches.

Next 2 rows: Bind off 4 (5, 6, 5) stitches, work in pattern as established—32 (34, 36, 38) stitches.

Bind off all remaining stitches for back neck.

Front

Work as for Back until piece measures 13½" [34.5cm] from eyelet hem, ending after working a WS row.

Fold Front in half, and place marker in the center for V-neck.

Decrease row (RS): Work in pattern to 4 stitches before marker, k2tog, k2, slip marker, join 2nd ball of yarn slip 1, k1, ssk, work in pattern to end—39 (43, 47, 51) stitches each side of neck. (**Note:** Slip 1st stitch at the

beginning of each row on the right and left sides of the garment to create neat edges.)

Next row: Purl.

Working both sides at the same time, repeat decrease row every 4th row 15 (16, 17, 18) times more—24 (27, 30, 33) stitches on each side of neck.

AT THE SAME TIME, when piece measures 14½" [37cm] from cast-on edge, begin armhole shaping as for Back, Shape Armholes.

AT THE SAME TIME, when armhole measures 7 (7¼, 7¾, 8)" [18 (18.5, 19.5, 20.5)cm], begin shoulder shaping as for Back, Shape Shoulders.

Finishing

Using a yarn needle, sew shoulder seams.

Neck Ruffle

With WS facing, starting at left shoulder seam, pick up and knit 2 stitches (from the back and front of each stitch) of bind-off row across the back neck, 2 stitches of each edge stitch down the Right Front and up the Left Front, count the stitches to make sure you have an even number, and join to work in the round.

Round 1: *K2tog, yo; repeat from * around.

Round 2: Knit.

Repeat last 2 rows 7 times more.

Bind off all stitches.

Sleeve Ruffle

With RS facing, place a marker 3½ (4, 4½, 5)" [9 (10, 11, 12.5)cm] down from shoulder seam on both front and back. Pick up and knit 2 stitches from each edge stitch between markers, making sure you have an even number.

Row 1 (WS): *P2, M1; repeat from * to end of picked up stitches. Turn.

Row 2 (RS) : *K2tog, yo; repeat from * to end of row, pick up and knit 2 additional stitches from sleeve edge. Turn.

Row 3: Purl to end of row, pick up and purl 2 additional stitches from sleeve edge. Turn.

Repeat last 2 rows 4 (4, 5, 5) times more.

Bind off all stitches.

Repeat for other armhole.

Sew side seams. Fold the lower edge to WS at eyelet hem row and sew in place, carefully matching knitting tension.

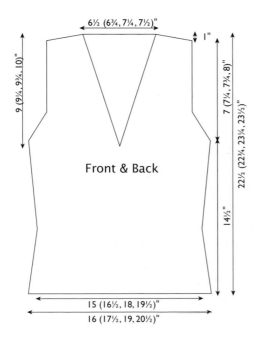

6½ (6¾, 7¼, 7½)"

1"

9 (9¼, 9¾, 10)"

7 (7¼, 7¾, 8)"

22½ (22¾, 23¼, 23½)"

14½"

Front & Back

15 (16½, 18, 19½)"

16 (17½, 19, 20½)"

NINOTCHKA SPAGHETTI-STRAP TANK

by Annie Modesitt

You shouldn't have to forgo the idea of a little spaghetti-strap tank top just because you're well-endowed. This one has a shelf bra inside! Short-row shaping and an elastic yarn for the bra, combined with a wide band of elastic sewn in at the bottom, will give you the beauty and support that you desire and deserve.

Skill Level
Intermediate

Sizes
XS (S, M, L, 1X, 2X)

Finished Measurements
Bust: 30 (34, 38, 42, 46, 50)" [76 (86.5, 96.5, 106.5, 117, 127)cm]
Length: 16 (17, 18, 19, 20, 21)" [40.5 (43, 45.5, 48, 51, 53.5)cm]

Materials
520 (780, 780, 780, 1040, 1040) yd [476 (714, 714, 714, 952, 952)m] / 2 (3, 3, 3, 4, 4) hanks Artyarns Silk Rhapsody (80% silk, 20% mohair, each approximately 3½ oz [100g] and 260 yd [238m]), in color #RH245 Raspberry Pink (A), **4** medium/worsted weight
200 (200, 200, 200, 300, 300) yd [184 (184, 184, 184, 276, 276)m] / 2 (2, 2, 2, 3, 3) balls Cascade Fixation (98.3% cotton, 1.7% elastic, each approximately 1¾ oz [50g] and 100 yd [92m]), in color #7219 Red (B), **2** fine/sport weight
326 yd [298m] / 2 hanks Artyarns Regal Silk 101 (100% silk, each approximately 1¾ oz [50g] and 163 yd [149m]), in color #RS245 Raspberry Pink (C), **2** fine/sport weight

312 (312, 624, 624, 624, 624) yd [285 (285, 570, 570, 570, 570)m] / 1 (1, 2, 2, 2, 2) hanks Artyarns Silk Mohair (60% mohair, 40% silk, each approximately 0.88 oz [25g] and 312 yd [285m]), in color #MS413 Pinks (D), **1** super fine/lace weight
260 yd [238m] / 1 hank Artyarns Silk Rhapsody (80% silk, 20% mohair, each approximately 3½ oz [100g] and 260 yd [238m]), in color #RH113 Browns (E), **4** medium/worsted weight
1 Size 5 [3.75mm] circular needle, 24" [61cm] long, or size needed to obtain gauge
1 Size 4 [3.5mm] circular needle, 24" [61cm] long
1 Size 8 [5mm] circular needle, 24" [61cm] long
Stitch markers
⅜" [9mm]-wide elastic, cut to rib cage measurement plus 2" [5cm]
Steam iron or garment steamer
Yarn needle
Sewing needle
Sewing thread

Gauge
24 stitches and 32 rows = 4" [10cm] over stockinette stitch using size 5 [3.75mm] circular needle

Instructions

Bodice
Using a provisional cast-on, with middle-size needle and A, cast on 180 (204, 228, 252, 276, 300) stitches.
Knit 2 rows. Join stitches to work in the round, placing marker to indicate beginning of round.
Eyelet round *K2tog, yo, k2; repeat from * around.
Next round: Purl.
Next round: Knit.
Work even in stockinette stitch until piece measures 7 (7½, 8, 8½, 9, 9½)" [18 (19, 20.5, 21.5, 23, 24)cm] from cast-on edge. Set work aside.

Shelf Bra
With smallest needles and B, cast on 168 (192, 216, 240, 264, 288) stitches.
Work back and forth in stockinette stitch for ½" [13mm], ending after working a RS row.
Next row (WS): Knit. Join stitches to work in the round, placing marker to indicate left side "seam."
Next round: (RS): *K2, p2; repeat from * around. Work even in 2x2 Rib (page **134**) for 1" [2.5cm].
Next round: *K15 (17, 19, 21, 23, 25), M1; repeat from * 6 times more (Front), place 2nd marker to indicate right side "seam," knit to end of round (Back)—180 (204, 228, 252, 276, 300) stitches.

Next round (Front short-row shaping): Knit to 2 stitches before 2nd marker; wrap and turn, work back to 2 stitches before 1st marker; wrap and turn.

Next round: Knit.

Repeat last 2 rounds until piece measures approximately 5⅛ (5⅛, 6⅛, 5¼, 6¼, 7¾)" [13 (13, 15.5, 13.5, 16, 19.5)cm] from cast-on edge of ribbing pattern when measured across the area without short rows (Back).

Note: For larger cup sizes, you may want to work some or all of the front short-row shaping again.

Join Bra to Bodice

Place pieces together with right sides facing. With middle-size needle and E, knit pieces together using the 3-needle bind-off.

Turn joined piece inside out so that the Shelf Bra is to the inside and the Bodice is facing out. Lightly steam-block the turning seam.

Top Edge Trim

With middle-size needle and E, pick up and knit 180 (204, 228, 252, 276, 300) stitches around top of work at join.

Knit 1 round.

Bind off all stitches using the I-cord bind-off.

Peplum

Slip provisional stitches onto a circular needle, and place marker to indicate center back.

Next round: With largest needle and C, *k15 (17, 19, 21, 23, 25) stitches, M1; repeat from * around 11 times more—192 (216, 240, 264, 288, 312) stitches.

Next round: Knit all stitches.

Rounds 1-6: Work Rows 1 and 2 of Lace Chart 3 times.

Rounds 7-10: Change to D and work Rows 3 and 4 of Lace Chart twice.

Repeat Rounds 1-10 until piece measures approximately 8 (8½, 9, 9½, 10, 10½)" [20.5 (21.5, 23, 24, 25.5, 26.5)cm].

Change to E and work Rounds 1-6 once more.

Knit 1 round.

Purl 1 round.

Bind off all stitches loosely.

Finishing

Steam-block piece through outer layer and
Shelf Bra.

Turn up bottom (stockinette stitch section) of
Shelf Bra. Using a yarn needle and B, sew in place
creating a casing. Slip the elastic into the casing
through the unjoined edge stitches from the 1st
rows of Shelf Bra. Using a sewing needle and
thread, tack ends of elastic together.

Try on top to determine length of shoulder ties
from top edge of Bodice to top of shoulder. With
E, make 2 Twisted Cord ties that measure twice
this length. Tack in place on front and back of
Bodice.

With E, make a Twisted Cord to measure around
the rib cage plus 8" [20.5cm]. Draw this cord
through eyelets at top of lace section, and
arrange cord so the ties hang down in the center
front.

With E, make a 10" [25.5cm] piece of I-cord. Tie
it into a bow and tack it to the I-cord bind-off at
the center front of the tank.

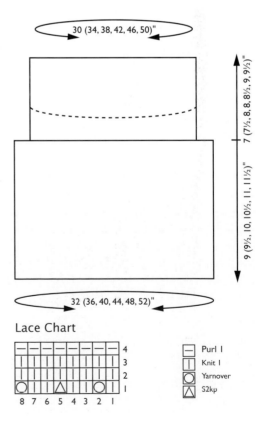

Lace Chart

| Purl 1 |
| Knit 1 |
| Yarnover |
| S2kp |

SHEILA'S TANK TOP

by Melissa Matthay

This body-hugging sweater is a more modest version of a bustier-style top, with a subtle chevron design. Knitted panels act as interfacing in the bust; most knitters will need only one pair, but you may need to make two or three.

Skill Level
Intermediate

Sizes
S (M, L, XL)

Finished Measurements
Bust: 18 (19½, 21, 22 22½)" [45.5 (49.5, 53.5, 57)cm]
Length: 18½ (20, 21½, 23)" [47 (51, 55, 58.5cm]

Materials
415 (415, 518, 664) yd5 (5, 7, 8) skeins Tahki Stacy Charles S. Charles Collection Venus (95% viscose, 5% polamide, each approximately 1¾ oz [50g] and 83 yd [75m], in color #38, **(4)** medium/worsted weight
1 Pair size 8 [5mm] needles

Gauge
16 stitches and 20 rows = 4" [10cm] over stockinette stitch using size 8 needles

Stitch Glossary
Stripe pattern
Rows 1 and 2: Knit.
Rows 3, 5, and 7: K2, yo, k to last 2 sts, yo, k2.
Rows 4, 6, and 8: Purl.
Row 9: Purl.
Row 10: Knit.
Repeat Rows 3–10 for pattern.

Chevron pattern
Rows 1 and 2: Knit.
Rows 3, 5, and 7: K2, yo, k15 (17, 19, 21), k2tog in back, k2, k2tog, k15 (17, 19, 21), yo, k2.
Rows 4, 6, and 8: Purl.
Row 9: Purl.
Row 10: Knit.
Repeat Rows 3–10 for pattern.

Instructions

Back
Cast on 60 (66, 72, 78) stitches. Work in stripe pattern until piece measures 12 (13, 14, 15)" [30.5 (33, 35.5, 38)cm].

Shape Armholes
Bind off 5 stitches at the beginning of the next 2 rows.
Decrease 1 stitch at each edge every other row 4 (5, 6, 7) times.
Work even until piece measures 18½ (20, 20½, 23)" [47 [51, 55, 58.5cm]. Bind off loosely.

Right Front
Cast on 40 (44, 48, 52) stitches. Work chevron pattern until piece measures 11 (12, 13, 14)" [28 (30.5, 33, 35.5)cm].

Left Front
Work as for Right Front.

Bust
Cast on 40 (42, 44, 46) stitches.
Row 1: K17 (18, 19, 20) stitches, k2tog in back, K2, k2tog, k17 (18, 19, 20) stitches.
Row 2 and all even rows: Knit.

Row 3: K16 (17, 18, 19) stitches, k2tog in back, k2, k2tog, k16 (17, 18, 19) stitches.
Row 5: K15 (16, 17, 18) stitches, k2tog in back, k2, k2tog, k15 (16, 17, 18) stitches.
Row 7: K14 (15, 16, 17) stitches, k2tog in back, k2, k2tog, k14 (15,16,17) stitiches.
Row 9: K13 (14, 15, 16) stitches, k2tog in back, k2, k2tog, k13 (14,15, 16) stitches. Continue decreasing in this manner until one stitch remains Bind off last stitch.

Finishing
Shoulder Straps
With right side facing, start at bottom of right front at the side seam. Pick up 20 (22, 24, 26) stitches from the outer edge of the bust.
Cast on 20 (22, 24, 16) stitches for the strap. Work in garter stitch for 2" [5cm]. Bind off very loosely.
Sew shoulders, center, and side seams together.

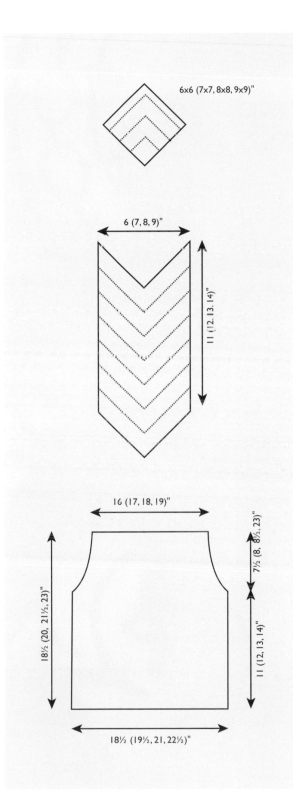

6x6 (7x7, 8x8, 9x9)"

6 (7, 8, 9)"

11 (12, 13, 14)"

16 (17, 18, 19)"

7½ (8, 8½, 23)"

18½ (20, 21½, 23)"

11 (12, 13, 14)"

18½ (19½, 21, 22½)"

NOTORIOUS LOW-CUT TOP

by Annie Modesitt

Some shapes deserve their moment in the sun—and this sweater shines with fitted detail! Horizontal I-cord adds a hint of underwire shaping, and ribbed sides and back emphasize waist shaping, exaggerating the curves of the bust and hips. The crocheted neck edging, twisted cord bust detail, and knit-on drape sleeves are worthy of a committed knitter. Loosen the front ties for a modest look, or tie them tight to create the illusion of cleavage.

Skill Level
Experienced

Sizes
XS (S, M, L, 1X, 2X)

Finished Measurements
Bust: 26½ (35, 39½, 44, 52½, 57)" [67.5 (89, 100, 112, 133.5, 145)cm]
Length: 22¾ (23¾, 24, 25, 26¼, 27½)" [58 (60, 61, 63.5, 66.5, 70)cm]

Materials
Berroco Touché (50% cotton, 50% Modal® rayon, each approximately 1¾ oz [50g] and 89 yd [82m]), (4) medium/worsted weight
356 (445, 445, 534, 623, 623) yd [328 (410, 410, 492, 574, 574)m] / 4 (5, 5, 6, 7, 7) hanks in color #7914 Lemon Meringue (A)
89 (178, 178, 178, 178, 178) yd [82 (164, 164, 164, 164, 164)m] / 1 (2, 2, 2, 2, 2) hanks in color #7930 Green Tea (B)

1 Size 8 [5mm] circular needle, 24" [61cm] long
1 Size 6 [4mm] circular needle, 24" [61cm] long
1 Size 7 [4.5mm] circular needle, 24" [61cm] long, or size to obtain gauge
1 Size F-5 [3.75mm] crochet hook
Stitch markers
Cable needle

Gauge
16 stitches and 24 rows = 4" [10cm] over 2x2 Rib (page **134**) using size 7 [4.5cm] circular needle

Stitch Glossary
Cable 4 left: Slip 2 stitches onto cable needle and hold to front, k2, k2 from cable needle.
Cable 4 right: Slip 2 stitches onto cable needle and hold to back, k2, k2 from cable needle.
Knit 3 together with a right slant: Knit 3 sts together as if they were 1 stitch.
Knit 3 together with a left slant: Knit 3 sts together through the back loop as if they were 1 stitch.

Instructions

Body

With largest needle and A, cast on 117 (157, 177, 197, 237, 257) stitches. Join stitches to work in the round, placing marker to indicate beginning of round.
Next round: Work Row 1 of Chart A (center cable) across 17 stitches between markers, and work Row 1 of Chart B (ribbing pattern) around remaining stitches 5 [7, 8, 9, 11, 12] times.
Next round: Work Row 2 of Chart A between markers as established, and work in ribbing

pattern as established around all remaining stitches.
Work in ribbing pattern as established, slipping markers in each round and working center 17 stitches in Chart A, until ribbing measures 1" [2.5cm] from cast-on edge.
Work 17 center stitches in cable as established, and work Rows 1 and 2 of Chart C (Bias Nondecrease Panel) around remaining stitches until piece measures 5½ (5½, 5¾, 5¾,

6, 6¼)" [14 (14, 14.5, 14.5, 15, 16)cm] from cast-on edge, ending after working Row 4 of Chart C.

Next round: Work 17 center stitches in Chart A as established, slip marker, work Row 1 of Chart D (Bias Decrease Panel) across next 20 stitches (shaping panel), place marker, repeat Row 1 of Chart C 3 [5, 6, 7, 9, 10] times, place marker, work Row 1 of Chart D across last 20 stitches (shaping panel).

Work center panel in cable as established, and work Charts C and D as established, working shaping only in panels on either side of cable with no shaping around sides and Back.

Decrease in shaping panels only as directed in chart to Row 18 of Chart D—101 (141, 161, 181, 221, 241) stitches.

Work even, repeat Rows 17 and 18 of Chart D in shaping panels with no further decreasing until piece measures 8⅝ (8⅝, 8¾, 8¾, 8⅞, 9)" [22 (22, 22.2, 22.2, 22.5, 23)cm] from cast-on edge.

Shape Upper Waist

Work to Row 36 of Chart D in shaping panels and work the 17 cable stitches and sides and Back in pattern as established—117 (157, 177, 197, 237, 257) stitches. With no further shaping, repeat Rows 1 and 2 of Chart C around all noncable stitches until piece measures 18¾ (19¼, 19½, 20, 20¾, 21½)" [47.5 (49, 49.5, 51, 53, 54.5)cm] from cast-on edge (or desired length to armholes), ending after working an even round, removing all markers in last round except for marker indicating beginning of round.

Divide for Front and Back
Shape Back Armholes

Next 2 rows: Working in pattern as established, bind off 5 (7, 8, 9, 11, 12) stitches, work in pattern as established.

Decrease 1 stitch at the beginning of each row 8 (11, 12, 14, 17, 18) times—32 (42, 48, 52, 62, 68) stitches across Back.

Work even until armhole measures 3½ (4, 4, 4½, 5, 5½)" [9 (10, 10, 11.5, 12.5, 14)cm] from cast-on edge of shaping.

Ruffled Crochet Edging

With B and crochet hook, work k2tog picot bind-off across all stitches, working 3 chains between each bound-off stitch. Do not cut yarn. (You will have a chain-3 space for each bound-off stitch, and the bind-off edge will look ruffled.) Turn work.

* Insert hook from WS to RS into next chain-3 space, bring hook from RS to WS back through next chain-3 space; repeat from * for next 2 chain-3 spaces—4 chain-3 spaces are resting on hook.

Draw a loop through all 4 chain spaces, chain 4 stitches, repeat from * across remaining chain-spaces. Fasten off.

Shape Front Armhole and Bust

Removing each marker as you come to it across the front, work horizontal I-cord across front 59 (79, 89, 99, 119, 129) stitches as follows:

Next row (RS): *K1 between next 2 stitches on needle, k2, ssk, slip 3 stitches from right-hand needle back onto left-hand needle; repeat from * until all stitches have been worked, ending after working ssk before double marker—59 (79, 89, 99, 119, 129) stitches across front.

Next row (WS): K29 (39, 44, 49, 59, 64) stitches, p1, knit to end.

Next row (RS): Pick up and knit edge stitch from right end of I-cord 2 rows below, purl next stitch on needle, pick up and knit from I-cord stitch next to a stitch just picked up (increase of 2 stitches), p2, knit to 1 stitch before center (knit) stitch, yo, s2kp, yo, knit to last 3 stitches, p2, pick up and knit edge stitch from left edge of I-cord, p1, pick up and knit from I-cord next stitch to 1 stitch just picked up (increase of 2 stitches)—63 (83, 93, 103, 123, 133) stitches.

Next row (WS): Slip 1 wyif, k1, slip 1 wyif, k2, purl to last 5 stitches, k2, slip 1 wyif, k1, slip 1 wyif.

Next row (RS): K1, slip 1 wyif, k1, knit to 1 stitch before center stitch, yo, S2KP, yo, knit to last 5 stitches, p2, k1, slip 1 wyif, k1.

Repeat last 2 rows until piece measures 6 (7¼, 7¾, 8½, 10, 10¾)" [15 (18.5, 19.5, 21.5, 25.5, 27.5)cm] from middle of horizontal I-cord band, ending after working a WS row.

Work Ruffled Crochet Edging across all stitches as for Back, working last ruffle with fewer than 3 chain-spaces if necessary.

Sleeve (Make 2)

With RS facing, smallest needle, and B, pick up and knit 23 (22, 22, 25, 27, 29) stitches up front armhole edge, use the cable cast-on method to cast on 20 (30, 30, 34, 34, 38) stitches, pick up and knit 17 (16, 16, 17, 19, 21) stitches down the back armhole edge—60 (68, 68, 76, 80, 88) stitches.

Next row (WS): Slip 1, wyif, k1, slip 1 wyif, k2 (edge), *k2, p2 repeat from * to last 5 stitches, ending k2, slip 1 wyif, k1, slip 1 wyif (edge).

Next row (RS): K1, slip 1 wyif, k1, p2 (edge), work 27 (31, 31, 35, 37, 41) stitches in pattern as established; wrap and turn.

Next row (WS): Work 4 stitches; wrap and turn.

Next row: Work to 3 stitches past last wrapped stitch; wrap and turn.

Change to middle-size needle. Repeat last row, working stitches together with their wraps, until all stitches are worked, ending after working a RS row.

Next row (WS): Work 32 (36, 36, 40, 42, 46) stitches in pattern as established; wrap and turn.

Next row (RS): Work 4 stitches; wrap and turn.

Next row: Work to 3 stitches past last wrapped stitch; wrap and turn.

Change to largest needle. Repeat last row until all stitches are worked at each edge, ending after working a WS row.

Knit next 2 rows.

Bind off all stitches loosely.

Finishing

Make a 40" [101.5cm] Twisted Cord (page **137**) using A and B.

Starting at the top center front, weave half of the cord down through the right bust eyelets and through loose stitches under the left cup. Repeat with other end of cord, weaving through the left bust eyelets and under the right cup.

Tack edges of cord to inside of Body.

Pull cord tight, gather it at the center Front bust, and tie it in a bow. Cut and knot the ends of the cord, leave it in a loop, or tuck it in as shown in the detail.

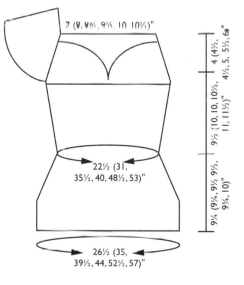

Chart A center cable
(work only across 17 sts)

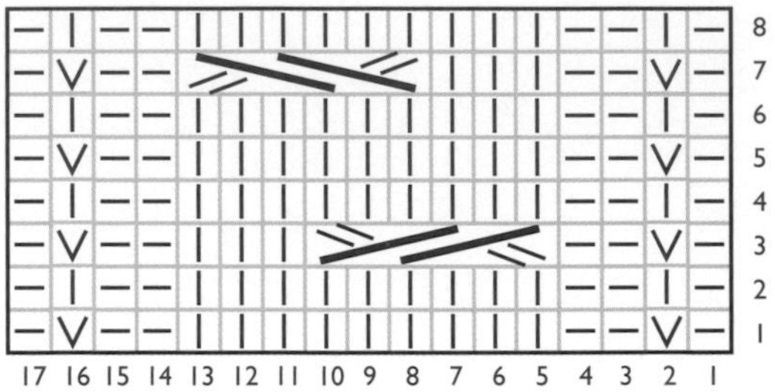

Chart B rib
(work across all noncenter Cable Chart sts)

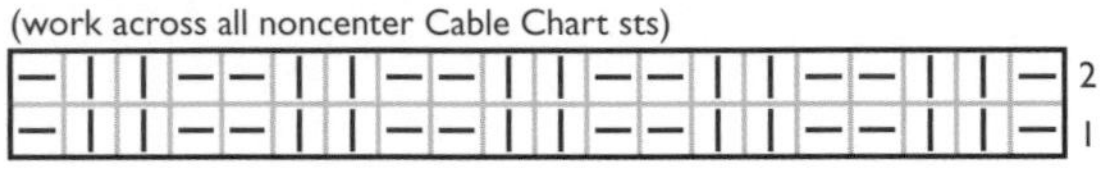

Chart C bias nondecrease panel
(repeat these 2 rows in all decreasing bias panels)

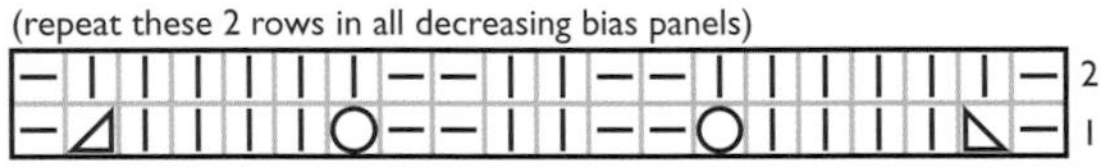

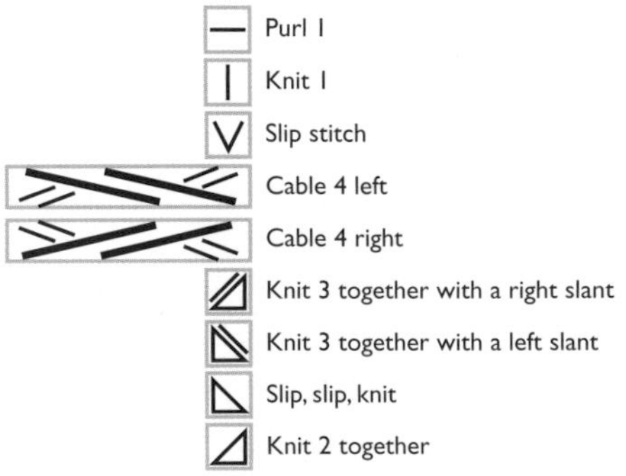
Purl 1
Knit 1
Slip stitch
Cable 4 left
Cable 4 right
Knit 3 together with a right slant
Knit 3 together with a left slant
Slip, slip, knit
Knit 2 together

Chart D bias decrease panel chart
(work only in panels on either side of center front Cable Chart))

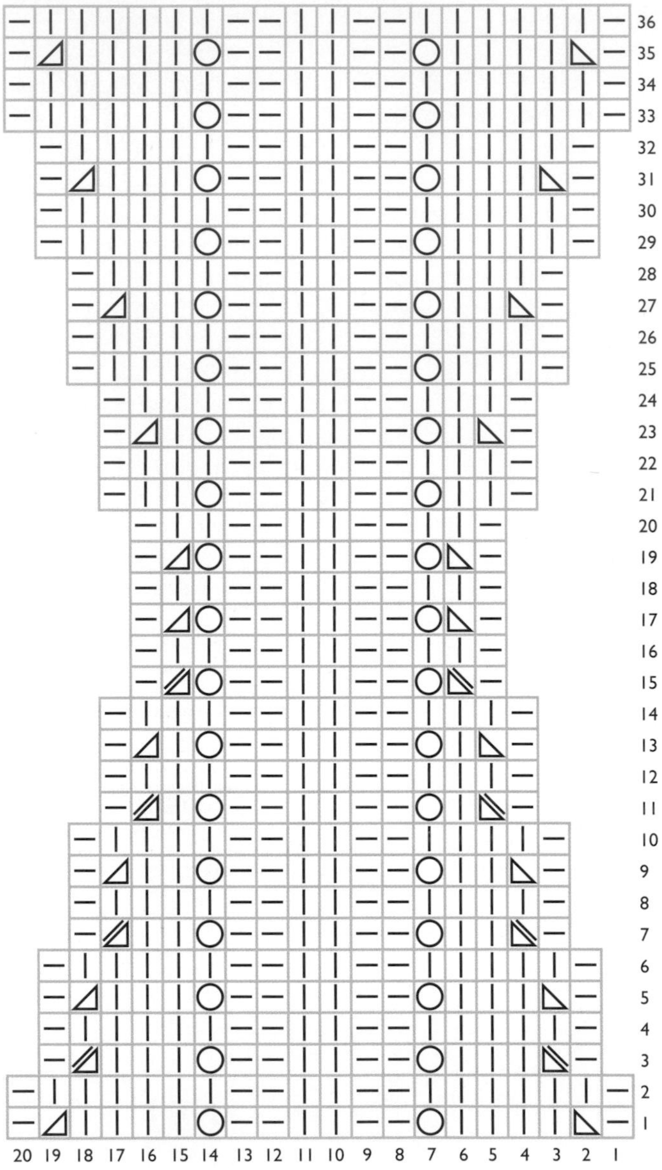

REBECCA'S TOP

by Melissa Matthay

This soft cotton tank is just a trifle flirty, with a beribboned empire waist setting off the lace-patterned bottom from the stockinette-knit top. Pop it over a camisole and wear it under a jacket when the occasion is sedate, or show some midriff on a night out with friends. The openwork lace pattern is a little tricky for beginners but a healthy challenge for experienced knitters.

Skill Level
Experienced

Sizes
S (M, L, XL)

Finished Measurements
Bust: 37 (40, 43, 46)" [94 (101.5, 109, 117)cm]
Length: 22½ (24, 25½, 26)" [57 (61, 64, 66)cm]

Materials
575 (690, 805, 920) yd [525 (630, 735, 840)m] /
5 (6, 7, 8) balls GGH Scarlett (100% cotton, each
approximately 1¾ oz [50g] and 115 yd [105m]),
in color #35 Turquoise, (**2**) fine/sport weight
1 Pair size 6 [4mm] needles, or size needed to
obtain gauge
1 Pair size 10 [6mm] needles, or size needed to
obtain gauge
1 Size 10 [6mm] circular needle, 16" [41cm] long
Yarn needle
2 yd [2m] Ribbon, ⅜" [9mm] wide

Gauge
19 stitches and 24 rows = 4" [10cm] over
stockinette stitch using size 6 [4mm] needles
and 1 strand of yarn

15 stitches and 18 rows = 4" [10cm] over
stockinette stitch using size 10 [6mm] needles
and 2 strands held together

Pattern Stitch
Lattice Lace (over a multiple of 13 stitches + 2)
Row 1 (RS): K1, *k2, skp, k4, k2tog, k2, yo, k1,
yo; repeat from * to last stitch, k1.
Row 2 and all WS rows: Purl.
Row 3: K1, *yo, k2, skp, k2, k2tog, k2, yo, k3;
repeat from * to last stitch, k1.
Row 5: K1, *k1, yo, k2, skp, k2tog, k2, yo, k4;
repeat from * to last stitch, k1.
Row 7: K1, *yo, k1, yo, k2, skp, k4, k2tog, k2;
repeat from * to last stitch, k1.
Row 9: K1, *k3, yo, k2, skp, k2, k2tog, k2, yo;
repeat from * to last stitch, k1.
Row 11: K1, *k4, yo, k2, skp, k2tog, k2, yo, k1;
repeat from * to last stitch, k1.
Row 12: Purl.
Repeat Rows 1–12 for Lattice Lace.

Instructions

Back
With smaller needles and 1 strand of yarn, cast on
93 (106, 106, 119) stitches.
Work even in Lattice Lace pattern until piece
measures 12 (13, 14, 14)" [30.5 (33, 35.5, 35.5)
cm] from cast-on edge, ending after working a
WS row.
Change to larger straight needles and 2 strands
of yarn.
Next row (RS): Knit across, decreasing 25 (32, 26,
33) stitches evenly spaced across—68 (74, 80,
86) stitches.

Beginning with a purl row, work even in
stockinette stitch for 1" [2.5cm], ending after
working a WS row.
Next row (RS): K1 *k2tog, yo; repeat from * to last
stitch, k1.
Beginning with a purl row, work even in
stockinette stitch until piece measures 15 (16,
17, 17)" [38 (40.5, 43, 43)cm] from cast-on edge,
ending after working a WS row.

Shape Armholes

Next 2 rows: Bind off 3 stitches, work in pattern as established—62 (68, 74, 80) stitches.

Decrease 1 stitch at each edge every other row 4 (5, 6, 7) times—54 (58, 62, 66) stitches.

Work even until piece measures 17 (18, 19, 19)" [43 (45.5, 48.5, 48.5)cm] from cast-on edge, ending after working a WS row.

Shape Neck

Next row (RS): K18 (19, 21, 22) stitches, join a 2nd ball of yarn, bind off center 18 (20, 20, 22) stitches, knit to end.

Working both sides at once, bind off 2 stitches at the beginning of each row 2 (1, 2, 2) times, then decrease 1 stitch every other row 3 (4, 3, 4) times. Work even on remaining 11 (13, 14, 14) stitches until armhole measures 7½ (8, 8½, 9)" [19 (20.5, 21.5, 23)cm], ending after working a WS row. Bind off all stitches on each side for shoulders.

Front

Work as for Back.

Finishing

Using a yarn needle, sew shoulder and side seams.

Neck Band

With RS facing, size 10 circular needle, and 2 strands of yarn, begin at left shoulder seam and pick up and knit 110 (114, 118, 122) stitches evenly spaced around neck edge.
Join and knit 1 row.
Bind off all stitches loosely knitwise.

Armbands

With RS facing, circular needle, and 2 strands of yarn, begin at underarm seam and pick up and knit 56 (62, 64, 66) stitches evenly spaced around armhole edge.
Join stitches to work in the round, and knit 1 row.
Bind off all stitches loosely knitwise.
Weave in drawstring ribbon.

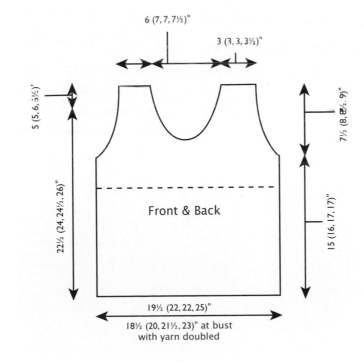

6 (7, 7, 7½)"

3 (3, 3, 3½)"

5 (5, 6, 6½)"

7½ (8, 8½, 9)"

22½ (24, 24½, 26)"

Front & Back

15 (16, 17, 17)"

19½ (22, 22, 25)"

18½ (20, 21½, 23)" at bust
with yarn doubled

MINI DRESS

by Caddy Melville Ledbetter

This long top looks just as great over pants or a skirt as it does over tights. And of course you can make it longer or shorter. The real fun, however, is not in the length (or lack thereof) but in the center and the sides. Even though there's shaping, the waist narrows visually because the center stripe is cut short by the vertical stripes at the sides.

Skill Level
Intermediate

Sizes
XS (S, M, L, XL)

Finished Measurements
Bust: 30½ (34½, 38½, 42½, 46½)" [77 (87.5, 97.5, 108, 118)cm]
Hem: 34 (38, 42, 46, 50)" [86.5 (96.5, 106.5, 117, 127)cm]
Length: 28 (28½, 29, 29½, 30)" [71 (72.5, 73.5, 75, 76)cm]
Waist length: 15½ (16, 16½, 17, 17½)" [39 (40.5, 42, 43, 44.5)cm]
Shoulder width: 12 (12½, 13½, 14½, 15½)" [30.5 (32, 34.5, 37, 39.5)cm]
Sleeve length: 9½ (9¾, 10¾, 11¾, 12¼)" [24 (25, 27.5, 30, 31)cm]

Materials
Louet Merlin (70% merino wool, 30% linen, each approximately 3½ oz [100g] and 156 yd [140m]), (4) medium/worsted weight
425 (465, 520, 565, 615) yd [385 (420, 470, 510, 555)m] / 3 (3, 4, 4, 4) skeins in color #43 Pewter (MC)
150 (155, 200, 250, 260) yd [135 (140, 180, 225, 235)m] / 1 (1, 2, 2, 2) skeins in color #49 Charcoal (A)

80 (80, 160, 240, 240) yd [72 (72, 145, 215, 215)m] / 1 (1, 2, 2) skeins in color #01 Champagne (B)
1 Pair size 8 [5mm] needles, or size needed to obtain gauge
Stitch holder
Yarn needle

Gauge
18 stitches and 24 rows = 4" [10cm] over stockinette stitch using size 8 [5mm] needles

Pattern Notes
This garment is long and shaped. Its finished length could be your ideal length for a Midlength Sweater, a Long Sweater, somewhere between the two, or longer than both. It is high-waisted, but you may adjust the Back Waist length (between the waist and the armhole) and Finished Garment length (between the waist and the hem) as indicated on page **12**.
Before you begin, divide color A and color B into 2 balls each (if you don't have 2 balls of each already).
Work in colors as established unless directed otherwise.
Twist the yarn when changing color by taking the color just worked over the next color.
Work all increases as lifted increases (page **136**).
The Sleeves are started from stitches picked up around the armhole and knit down to the cuff.

Instructions

Front

With MC, use the long-tail cast-on method to cast on 79 (88, 97, 106, 115) stitches.

Knit 1 row.

Purl 1 row.

Knit 1 row.

Next row (RS): In color A k6 (6, 8, 10, 10), in color B k2 (2, 4, 6, 6), in MC k63 (72, 73, 74, 83), in color B k2 (2, 4, 6, 6), in color A k6 (6, 8, 10, 10).

Next row (WS): Purl in colors as established.

Repeat last 2 rows twice more, ending after working a WS row.

*Decrease row (RS):** K9 (9, 13, 17, 17), skp, knit to last 3 stitches in MC, k2tog, knit to end.

Work 7 rows even. (Shorten or lengthen the Finished Garment length here, page **12**, by changing the number of rows worked even between decreases.)

Repeat from * 7 times more, then repeat decrease row—61 (70, 79, 88, 97) stitches.

Next row: Purl in colors as established. (Piece measures approximately 12½" [32cm].)

Waist Stripe

Next row (RS): K8 (8, 12, 16, 16), in color B knit center 45 (54, 55, 56, 65) stitches, k8 (8, 12, 16, 16).

Next row (WS): P8 (8, 12, 16, 16), in color B purl center 45 (54, 55, 56, 65) stitches, p8 (8, 12, 16, 16).

Repeat last 2 rows until waist stripe measures 2" [5cm], ending after working a WS row.

Next row (RS): K8 (8, 12, 16, 16) stitches, in MC k45 (54, 55, 56, 65), k8 (8, 12, 16, 16).

Next row (WS): Purl.

Increase row (RS): K9 (9, 13, 17, 17), increase 1, knit to last 2 stitches in MC, increase 1, knit to end.

Work 5 rows even.

Repeat the last 6 rows 4 times more—71 (80, 89, 98, 107) stitches. (Shorten or lengthen the Back Waist length here, page **12**, by changing the number of rows worked even between increases.)

Work even until piece measures 6" [15cm] from top of waist stripe, ending after working a WS row.

Shape Armholes

Next 2 rows: Bind off 3 (4, 6, 8, 8) stitches, work in pattern as established—65 (72, 77, 82, 91) stitches.

1st decrease row (RS): K2 (2, 4, 6, 6), skp (in color B), knit to last 4 (4, 6, 8, 8) stitches, k2tog (in color B), knit to end.

(**Note:** There is only 1 stitch in color B at each side from here to end.)

Next row and all subsequent WS rows: Purl.

2nd decrease row (RS): K3 (3, 3, 5, 5), skp (in MC), knit to last 5 (5, 5, 7, 7) stitches, k2tog (in MC), knit to end.

3rd decrease row (RS): K3 (3, 2, 4, 4), skp, knit to last 5 (5, 4, 6, 6) stitches, k2tog, knit to end.

4th decrease row (RS): K3 (3, 3, 3, 3), skp, knit to last 5 (5, 5, 5, 5) stitches, k2tog, knit to end.

5th decrease row (RS): K3 (3, 3, 4, 4), skp, knit to last 5 (5, 5, 6, 6) stitches, k2tog, knit to end.

Next row (WS): Purl.

Repeat the last 2 rows 0 (2, 2, 2, 5) times more— 55 (58, 63, 68, 71) stitches, ending after working a WS row. (Adjust the Shoulder width here, page **15**.)

Work even until armhole measures 2½ (3, 3½, 4, 4½)" [6.5 (7.5, 9, 10, 11.5)cm], ending after working a WS row.

Shape Neck

Next row (RS): K9 (10, 12, 14, 15), slip these stitches to a stitch holder, bind off center 37 (38, 39, 40, 41) stitches, k9 (10, 12, 14, 15).

Next row (WS): Beginning with a purl row, work even in stockinette stitch until neck measures 5" [12.5cm]. Bind off all stitches.

Slip stitches from the stitch holder to a working needle, ready to work a WS row.

Beginning with a purl row, work even in stockinette stitch until neck measures 5" [12.5cm].

Bind off all stitches.

Back

Work as for Front to Shape Neck, but work until armhole measures 4½ (5, 5½, 6, 6½)" [11.5 (12.5, 14, 15, 16.5)cm], ending after working a WS row.

Next row (RS): K9 (10, 12, 14, 15), place these stitches on a holder, bind off center 37 (38, 39, 40, 41) stitches (for Back neck), k9 (10, 12, 14, 15).

Slip stitches from the stitch holder to a working needle, ready to work a WS (purl) row. Work even in stockinette stitch until the neck measures 3" [7.5cm].

Bind off all stitches.

Finishing

Block both pieces to finished measurements. Using a yarn needle, sew right shoulder seam.

Neck Edging

With RS facing and MC, beginning at left Front neck edge, pick up and knit 1 stitch for every 2 rows and 1 stitch for every stitch around entire neck edge.

Knit 1 row.

Purl 1 row.

Bind off all stitches.

Sew left shoulder and edging seam.

Sleeve (Make 2)

With RS facing and A, beginning at underarm seam, pick up and knit 1 stitch for every bind-off stitch, and 1 stitch for every 2 rows around entire armhole edge—51 (56, 63, 70, 73) stitches. (If needed, increase or decrease in the next row to attain the correct number for your size.)

Next row (WS): Purl.

Next row (RS): Bind off 3 stitches, knit to end.

Next row: Bind off 3 stitches, purl to end.

Next row (RS): Bind off 2 stitches, knit to end.

Next row: Bind off 2 stitches, purl to end.

Repeat the last 2 rows 5 (5, 6, 7, 7) times more—21 (26, 29, 32, 35) stitches, ending after working a WS row.

Next 2 rows: Bind off 6 (7, 8, 9, 10) stitches, work in pattern as established—9 (12, 13, 14, 15) stitches.

Bind off all stitches.

Sleeve Edging

With RS facing and A, beginning at an underarm seam, pick up and knit 1 stitch for every bind-off stitch around entire Sleeve edge—51 (53, 60, 70, 73) stitches.

WS row: Knit.

RS row: Purl.

Bind off all stitches.

Block Sleeves.

Using a yarn needle, sew Sleeve and edging together at underarm.

Sew side seams.

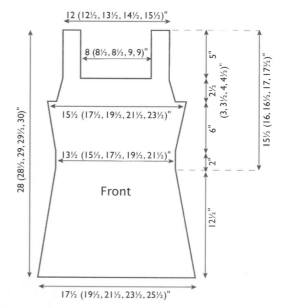

12 (12½, 13½, 14½, 15½)"

8 (8½, 8½, 9, 9)"

5"

2½ (3, 3½, 4, 4½)"

15½ (16, 16½, 17, 17½)"

15½ (17½, 19½, 21½, 23½)"

6"

13½ (15½, 17½, 19½, 21½)"

2"

28 (28½, 29, 29½, 30)"

Front

12½"

17½ (19½, 21½, 23½, 25½)"

AUDREY PULLOVER

by Mary Weaver

With a classic round yoke neckline, the Audrey pullover lives up to its impeccably polished namesake. Tailored darts enhance the sophisticated silhouette of this timeless sweater, while a row of bright blue buttons adds a playful touch.

Skill Level
Intermediate

Sizes
XS (S, M, L, XL)

Finished Measurements
Bust: 30 (34, 38, 42, 46)" [76 (86.5, 96.5, 106.5, 117)cm]
Length: Adjustable. This sweater is knit from the bottom up, so join the sleeves when it is long enough to fit.
Upper arm: 9½ (10, 11, 11½, 13)" [24 (25.5, 28, 29, 33)cm]

Materials
984 (1230, 1476, 1599, 1845) yd [904 (1130, 1356, 1469, 1695)m] / 8 (10, 12, 13, 15) balls Knit Picks CotLin (70% tanguis cotton, 30% linen, each approximately 1¾ oz [50g] and 123 yd [113m]), in color Pomegranate, **(3)** light/DK weight

1 Size 6 [4mm] circular needle, 24" [61cm] long, or size needed to obtain gauge
1 Set of 5 size 6 [4mm] double-pointed needles
1 Size D-3 [3.25mm] crochet hook
Stitch markers (one a different color)
Stitch holders (scrap yarn)
Yarn needle
Sewing needle
Sewing thread
6 Buttons, ½" [13mm] wide

Gauge
22 stitches and 30 rounds = 4" [10 cm] over stockinette stitch using size 6 [4mm] needle

Pattern Note
This sweater is meant to fit closely. When choosing your size, go for the one with the least ease or, if necessary, a little bit of negative ease.

Instructions

Body

With circular needle, cast on 164 (188, 208, 232, 254) stitches. Place marker and join stitches to work in the round, being careful not to twist stitches on needle.

Work in a 2x2 Rib (page **134**) for 1" [2.5cm].

Next round: K19 (22, 25, 28, 30), place marker, k44 (50, 54, 60, 67), place marker, k38 (44, 50, 56, 60), place marker, k44 (50, 54, 60, 67), place marker, knit to end. (**Note:** These markers establish the placement of waist darts on the sweater, so make sure that they are distinct from the beginning-of-the-round marker.)

Knit 4 (3, 3, 4, 4) rounds.

Decrease round: Knit to 1st marker, slip marker, ssk, knit to 2 stitches before 2nd marker, k2tog, slip marker, knit to 3rd marker, slip marker, ssk, knit to 2 stitches before 4th marker, k2tog, slip marker, knit to end.

Repeat the last 5 (4, 4, 5, 5) rounds 7 (10, 10, 10, 10) times more—132 (144, 164, 188, 210) stitches.

Work even in stockinette stitch (knit every round) for 1" [2.5cm].

Increase round: Knit to 1st marker, slip marker, k1, M1, knit to 1 stitch before 2nd marker, M1, k1, slip marker, knit to 3rd marker, slip marker, k1, M1, knit to 1 stitch before 4th marker, M1, k1, slip marker, knit to end.

Knit 4 (3, 3, 4, 4) rounds.

Repeat the last 5 (4, 4, 5, 5) rounds 7 (10, 10, 10, 10) times more—164 (188, 208, 232, 254) stitches.

Next round: Knit to end, removing dart placement markers as you come to them.

Work even in stockinette stitch until piece reaches approximately 1" [2.5cm] below underarm, when tried on with the smallest, middle region of the darts centered at the waist. Set aside.

Sleeve (Make 2)

With double-pointed needles, cast on 52 (52, 56, 64, 72) stitches and divide stitches evenly over 4 needles. Join stitches to work in the round, taking care not to twist stitches on needles, and place marker for the beginning of the round.
Work in a 2x2 Rib for 3" [7.5cm].
Knit 11 rounds.
Increase round: K1, M1, knit to 1 stitch from end of round, M1, k1—54 (54, 58, 66, 74) stitches.

Sizes S and M Only

Repeat the last 12 rounds once more—56 (60) stitches.

For All Sizes

Work even in stockinette stitch on 54 (56, 60, 64, 74) stitches until piece measures 7½ (8, 8, 8½, 8½)" [19 (20.5, 20.5, 21.5, 21.5)cm] from cast-on edge.
Next round: Knit to 6 (7, 8, 9, 10) stitches from end of round, place next 12 (14, 16, 18, 20) stitches on scrap yarn for underarm, and slip the remaining 42 (42, 44, 48, 54) stitches onto a stitch holder for Sleeve.
Cut yarn, leaving a 12" [30.5cm] tail. Set aside.

Yoke

Return to Body stitches and remove beginning-of-round marker.
Next round: K6 (7, 8, 9, 10), place marker, *slip 70 (80, 88, 98, 107) stitches, transfer next 12 (14, 16, 18, 20) stitches to scrap yarn for underarm; repeat from * once more to end at the beginning of the round.

Join Body and Sleeves

Next round: *Knit to 1 stitch before held section, knit next stitch together with 1st stitch of 1st Sleeve, knit to 1 stitch before last stitch of Sleeve, knit last stitch of Sleeve together with next stitch of Body; repeat from * once more, removing beginning-of-round marker and replacing it after the last Sleeve stitch is worked together with a Body stitch—220 (240, 260, 288, 318) stitches.

Size XL Only

Next round: *K157, k2tog; repeat from * once more—316 stitches.

For All Sizes

Work even in stockinette stitch on 220 (240, 260, 288, 316) stitches until piece measures 1" [2.5cm] from the join of Body and Sleeves. The sweater is worked back and forth in rows (not in the round) from here on.

Next row (RS): Slip 2 stitches wyib, knit to end. Turn work.

Next row (WS): Slip 2 stitches wyif, purl to end. Repeat the last 2 rows until piece measures 3" [7.5cm] from the join of Body and Sleeves, ending after working a WS row.

Next row (RS): Slip 2 stitches wyif, *k2, k2tog; repeat from * across to last 2 stitches, k2—166 (181, 196, 217, 238) stitches.

Keeping the 2 slipped stitches at the edges, work even in stockinette stitch until piece measures 6" [15cm] from the join of Body and Sleeves, ending after working a WS row.

Next row (RS): Slip 2 stitches wyib, *k1, k2tog; repeat from * across to last 2 stitches, k2—112 (122, 132, 146, 160) stitches.

Sizes S and L Only

Next row (WS): Slip 2 wyif, p1, p2tog, purl to last 5 stitches, p2tog, p3—120 (144) stitches.

For All Sizes

Work 1 (0, 1, 0, 1) row even.

Keeping the 2 slipped stitches at the edges, work in 2x2 Rib on 112 (120, 132, 144, 160) stitches for 1" [2.5cm].

Bind off all stitches in pattern.

Finishing

Transfer each group of underarm stitches from scrap yarn back to double-pointed needles. Graft corresponding stitches using a yarn needle and Kitchener Stitch, making sure to close any holes at each side of grafted seam.

Button Loops

With RS facing and crochet hook, make 8 evenly spaced button loops along right front edge of yoke split.

Using a sewing needle and thread, sew buttons to left edge of yoke split, opposite button loops.

20½ (22, 24, 26, 29)"

10 (10¾, 11, 12, 13½)"

30 (34, 38, 42, 46)"

7½ (8, 8, 8½, 8½)"

24 (26, 30, 34, 38)"

ABBREVIATIONS

3-NEEDLE BO: 3-needle bind-off

BEG: Beginning

BO: Bind off/bind-off

CC: Contrasting color

CCO: Cable cast-on

CIRC: Circular

CN: Cable needle

CO: Cast on/cast-on

DEC: Decrease

DPN: Double-pointed needles

EST: Established

FOLL: Following, follows

INC: Increase

K: Knit stitch

K1: Knit 1 stitch

K1TBL: Knit 1 stitch through the back loop

K2TOG: Knit 2 stitches together

K2TOGR: Knit 2 stitches together with right slant

K2TOG PICOT BO: Knit 2 together picot bind-off

LH: Left hand needle

M1: Make 1 stitch.

MC: Main color

P: Purl stitch

P1: Purl 1

P1TBL: Purl 1 stitch through the back loop

P2TOG: Purl 2 stitches together

P2TOG TBL: Turn the work over slightly and insert the needle from the left-hand side into the back loops of the second and the first stitches, in that order, then wrap the yarn around the needle in front to complete the purl stitch

P3TOG: Purl 3 stitches together

PATT: Pattern

PM: Place marker

PSSO: Pass slipped stitch over

PU&K: Pick up and knit

RH: Right-hand needle

REV ST ST: Reverse Stockinette stitch

SL: Slip

ST(S): Stitch(es)

ST ST: Stockinette stitch

TBL: Through the back loop

TW1: Twist 1 stitch

VDD: Vertical double decrease

W&T: Wrap and turn

WYIF: With yarn in front

WYIB: With yarn in back

YO: Yarn over

GLOSSARY

* ASTERISK: Repeat instructions following the single asterisk as directed.

1 x 1 RIB: Also known as K1, P1 Rib (KNIT ONE, PURL ONE RIBBING). Any odd number of stitches. Row 1 (RS): Knit one, *purl one, knit one; repeat from * to end. Row 2: Purl one, *knit one, purl one; repeat from * to end. Repeat rows 1 and 2.

2X2 RIB: Also known as K2, P2 RIB (KNIT TWO, PURL TWO RIBBING). Multiple of 4 stitches + 2 extra. Row 1 (RS): Knit two, *purl two, knit two; repeat from * to end. Row 2: Purl two, *knit two, purl two; repeat from * to end. Repeat rows 1 and 2.

3-NEEDLE BIND-OFF: The 3-needle bind-off is a great way to both bind off and seam and the same time. It is often used for the shoulder seams of sweaters. Step 1: With the right side of the two pieces facing each other, and the needles parallel, insert a third needle knitwise into the first stitch of each needle, wrap the yarn around the needle as if to knit. Knit these two stitches together and slip them off the needles. Step 2: Knit the next two stitches together from each needle in the same way as in Step 1. Step 3: Slip the first stitch on the third needle over the second stitch and off the needle. Repeat steps 2 and 3 across the row until all the stitches are bound off.

BACKWARD LOOP (E) INCREASE: *Wrap the working yarn around left thumb in a clockwise direction so the yarn coming from the needle is on top of the yarn circled around the thumb; insert the right needle under the yarn circle to the outside thumb, then slip the new stitch to right needle. Repeat from * for each increase.

BIND OFF/BIND-OFF (BO): The basic last step to complete to get the stitches of your project off the needles by making a finished edge.

BLOCKING: The process of wetting, steaming or spraying (misting) to stretch and shape a finished knitted piece to reach the dimensions suggested in the pattern, to make two pieces that need to match the same size, or to make your stitches look more even. The decision about how to block your pieces depends on the content of the yarn and the type of stitch pattern. Understanding the properties of the yarns used will help decide on how to block. Always read the yarn's ball band carefully before proceeding to know the important information about the care of the yarn.

CABLE 4 LEFT (C4L): Also known as CABLE 4 FRONT (C4F). Slip 2 stitches onto cable needle, knit 2 sts, bring slipped stitches to front of work and knit them.

CABLE 4 RIGHT (C4R): Also known as CABLE 4 BACK (C4B). Slip 2 stitches onto cable needle, knit 2 stitches, bring slipped stitches to back of work and knit them.

CABLE CAST-ON (CCO): Adjust work so that all stitches are on the left-hand needle. Slip needle between first and second sts on left-hand needle and pull loop through to front. Slip this loop onto the left-hand needle, twisting it clockwise. Repeat, each time using new st as new first stitch on left-hand needle.

CABLE NEEDLE (CN): Short knitting needle, used as an aid in the twisting of a cable.

CHANGE TO SMALLER OR LARGER NEEDLES: Sometimes different-sized needles are used in different parts of a project. The pattern will tell you when to use the different sizes.

E WRAP CAST-ON: With both tail and needle in the left hand, *take the right index finger under the working yarn (from back to front), turn the finger 180 degrees to the left, then insert the needle through the loop on the finger. Repeat from *.

GARTER STITCH: Works on any number of stitches. In flat knitting: Knit (or purl) every row. In circular knitting: Knit one round, purl the next round.

I-CORD: Cast on 3, 4, 5 or 6 stitches using double-pointed needles. Step 1: Knit, do not turn. Step 2: Slide the stitches back to the beginning of the needle. Repeat steps one and two until you have a short length of knitting, pulling down on the cord and the gap at the back will close. Repeat until the cord is the length you desire. Thread the yarn through the stitches and pull firmly.

I-CORD BIND-OFF: Also known as APPLIED I-CORD, I-cord that is worked on the bind-off row. This makes a decorative edging that is firm and has a nicely finished appearance. Cast on 3 stitches, using the cable cast-on. Step 1: Knit 2 stitches, and then knit 2 stitches together through the back loop (K2tog tbl). Step 2: Slip the 3 worked stitches back onto the left-hand needle, then pull the working yarn tightly across the back of those 3 stitches. Repeat steps 1 and 2. The result is a raised I-cord edging running perpendicular to the body of knitting.

I-CORD HORIZONTAL STRIPE: (Cast on 1 stitch using cable cast-on, keep the new stitch on your right-hand needle. Knit 2, knit 2 together left. Slip 3 stitches from right-hand needle back onto the left-hand needle. Repeat across work until all stitches are worked.

K1 (KNIT ONE STITCH): Create a stitch by inserting the needle through the stitch from the front to the back, wrapping yarn around the needle and pulling loop through.

K1TBL: (KNIT ONE STITCH THROUGH BACK LOOP): Also known as KTBL. Insert the right needle into the back of the stitch from the front to back and knit the stitch.

K2TOG (KNIT TWO STITCHES TOGETHER) (over 2 stitches): Also known as K2TOGR. This is a right-slanting, single decrease when used on the right side of the work. Knit 2 stitches together as though they were 1 stitch.

K2TOG PICOT BO (KNIT TWO TOGETHER PICOT BIND OFF): This can also be worked with a crochet hook in lieu of the left-hand needle to add picot chain stitches to the k2tog bind off. Step 1: Knit 2 stitches

together left (K2togL or K2tog tbl), and slip the stitch created back onto the left needle. Step 2: Knit this stitch, then slip the stitch just created back onto the left-hand needle (repeat once or as many times as required for picot chain). Repeat steps 1 and 2 along row until the last two stitches, knit 2 stitches together left, fasten off.

K2TOGR (KNIT 2 STITCHES TOGETHER WITH RIGHT SLANT)(over 2 stitches): Also known as K2TOG. This is a double decrease when used on the right side of the work. Knit 2 stitches together as if they were 1 stitch.

KF&B (KNIT INTO THE FRONT AND BACK OF ONE STITCH) INCREASE: Also known as KFB or BAR INCREASE. On a knit row, knit first into the front of the stitch normally, then, before slipping it off the needle, knit again into the back of the same stitch, and slip the stitch off. The same method is applied to a purl row; in this case, you purl into the front then the back of the stitch.

KITCHENER STITCH: Also known as GRAFTING. Preparation: Cut the yarn that you have been knitting with, leaving a long tail. Thread the tail onto a yarn needle. Place the needles with the stitches on them on top of each other, so that the wrong sides of the work are facing in toward each other. Slide the yarn needle through the first stitch on the front needle as if to purl, leaving the stitch on the needle and pulling the yarn snug all the way through the stitch. Now take the needle and slide it through the first stitch on the back needle as if to knit, again not slipping the stitch off the needle and pulling the yarn snug all the way through the stitch. Now you are ready to begin the grafting. Step 1: Slide the yarn needle into the first stitch on the front needle as if to knit, this time slipping the stitch off the knitting needle and pulling tight. Step 2: The now first stitch on the front needle is stitched next, with the yarn needle going in as if to purl, and without slipping the stitch off the needle. Pull the yarn all the way through. Step 3: Slide yarn needle into the first stitch on the back needle as if to purl and slide that stitch off the needle and pull snug. Step 4: Slide the yarn needle into what is now the first stitch on the back needle as if to knit, leaving the stitch on the needle. As usual, pull the yarn all the way through. Steps 1 to 4 complete one round of Kitchener Stitch. Repeat steps 1 to 4 on each of the following stitches.

KNITWISE: Also known as K-WISE or AS IF TO KNIT. Insert right needle into the stitch as if to knit it.

LIFTED INCREASE: This is a right-slanting increase. Insert right needle downward into the back of the stitch (the purl nub) in the row below the first stitch on left-hand needle, and knit, then knit the stitch on the needle.

LONG-TAIL CAST-ON: Also known as DOUBLE CAST-ON or 2-STRAND CAST-ON. Step 1: Place a slipknot several inches into a strand of yarn (roughly 1" [2.5 cm] for each stitch to be cast on). Place the slipknot on a knitting needle and hold the needle in your right hand. Be sure to keep the tail toward you and the live end of the yarn away from you. Step 2: With the needle in your right hand, slip your left thumb and index finger between the two strands of yarn and separate them. Hold both strands of yarn securely in your left hand. Step 3: Spread your thumb and index finger and turn your palm upward. Touch the tip of your needle to your palm and slide the needle up your thumb, under the yarn. Step 4: Move the tip of the needle toward your index finger and grab the strand that is wrapped around that finger. Return to the thumb and slide the tip of the needle back down the thumb toward the palm. Step 5: Allow the loop around your thumb to slip off, separating the two strands to tighten the cast-on stitch just created. Repeat steps 2 to 5 for desired number of stitches to cast on.

M1 (MAKE ONE STITCH): This is a single increase. It utilizes the running thread between 2 live stitches to create a new stitch. This increase can lean to the left (M1L) or to the right (M1R) depending on which direction you pick up the new stitch. If the method is not specified, use whichever increase you like.

P1 (PURL ONE STITCH): Create a stitch by inserting the needle through the stitch from the back to the front, wrapping yarn around the needle and pulling loop back through.

P2TOG (PURL TWO STITCHES TOGETHER) (over 2 stitches): This is a right-slanting, single decrease. Purl two stitches together as though they were one stitch.

PROVISIONAL CAST-ON: Also known as INVISIBLE CAST-ON. The waste yarn used can be pulled out later to continue the knitting in the opposite direction. Holding the ends of a waste yarn and the working yarn, make an overhand knot. Place a needle held in the left hand between the two yarns, with the knot below, the waste yarn held underneath and parallel to the needle out to the right, and the working yarn up and in front of the needle. Bring the working yarn down behind the needle and in front of the waste yarn; up behind the waste yarn and over-and-up then down in front of the needle; down behind the waste yarn; then up in front of the needle. Repeat for each two stitches. When desired number of stitches is reached, loosely fasten the waste yarn and work as usual with the working yarn. To take out the provisional cast-on, unfasten the end of the waste yarn and carefully pull it out, picking up the now loose loops on a needle and working from the opposite direction of previous work.

PU&K (PICK UP AND KNIT): Insert needle into fabric, wrap yarn around tip of needle and draw through fabric.

PURLWISE: Also known as P-WISE or AS IF TO PURL. Insert right needle down into the front loop, or up into the back loop for tbl (through back loop).

REVERSE STOCKINETTE STITCH: In flat knitting: Purl on right side; knit on wrong side. In circular knitting: Purl every round on right side.

RIB: Also known as RIBBING. Vertical columns of knit and purl stitches, side by side, as in K1, P1 knitting.

RS (RIGHT SIDE): The outside or public side of a sweater. Also stated to indicate which side is facing you when carrying out instructions.

S2KP (SL1-K2TOG-PSSO) (over 3 stitches): This is a left-slanting double decrease when used on the right side of the work. Slip one stitch knitwise, knit 2 stitches together, and pass the slipped stitch over the two stitches knitted together.

SELVEDGE: Also known as SELVAGE. All knitting has a selvedge on each side—the first and last stitches. If there is seaming, these are the stitches that will be used to seam the piece together; they will no longer be visible when it is sewn. With knitting projects such as scarves and afghans there are no seams, but only selvedge. Sometimes a pattern will tell you to work the first and last stitch in a specific way, such as slipping the first stitch and knitting the last stitch. This creates a neat selvedge on each side that enhances the look of the project.

SLIP (SL): Stitches are slipped without working from the right needle to the left needle. They can be slipped either purlwise or knitwise. If the pattern instructions do not specify which way, slip the stitch or stitches purlwise. If slipping stitch(es) when decreasing and instructions do not specify, then slip it knitwise on the knit rows, and purlwise on the purl rows.

SKP: Slip 1 knitwise, knit 1, pass the slip stitch over—1 stitch decreased with a right-side, left-slanting decrease.

SSK: Slip the next 2 stitches, one-at-a-time and knitwise from the left needle onto the right, insert the left needle into the front of the two stitches, and knit them together—1 stitch decreased with a right-side, left-slanting decrease.

SSP: Slip the next 2 stitches one-at-a-time and knitwise from the left needle onto the right, pass the slipped stitches back onto the left needle, purl these 2 stiches together through the back—1 stitch decreased with a right-side, left-slanting decrease.

STOCKINETTE STITCH (ST ST): In flat knitting: Knit on right side, purl on the wrong side. In circular knitting: Knit every round on the right side.

TW1 (TWIST 1 STITCH): When working this stitch, insert the needle into the stitch so that the stitch twists (tightens) as it is worked. This is used to close yarn overs and to create twisted rib (also known as k1tbl).

TWISTED CORD: Measure a length of yarn 4 times longer than the desired length of the cord. Fold the strand in half and make a slipknot at the cut ends. Pass the slipknot over a doorknob and stand far enough away that the yarn hangs in mid-air and does not touch the ground. Slip a crochet hook into the loop you are holding in your hand and pull the cord taut so that the hook rests perpendicular to your fingers, allowing the hook to slip between your middle and pointer finger. Begin turning the hook—similar to the way that the propeller on a toy airplane twists a rubber band—to twist the strands of yarn. Continue twisting until the yarn is quite taut and evenly twisted. When relaxed slightly, the twisted yarn will want to kink up. Still holding one end of the yarn in your left hand, with your right hand pinch the twisted strand midway between yourself and the doorknob. Bring the ends of the yarn together by moving toward the doorknob, but do not let go of the middle of the twisted yarn. When the piece is folded in half, release the middle of the cord. You will notice the yarn twisting around itself, forming a plied cord. Still holding tightly to the looped end, loosen the slipknot end from the doorknob and tie both ends together. Run your finger between the cords to even out the twists if necessary.

VDD (VERTICAL DOUBLE DECREASE) (over 3 stitches): Also known as CDD (CENTER DOUBLE DECREASE) or SL2–K1–P2SSO (S2KP2). This is a centered, double decrease. Slip two stitches together knitwise, knit one stitch, and pass the two slipped stitches together over the knitted stitch and off the right–hand needle.

W&T (WRAP AND TURN): This is the most common way of creating short rows. Bring the yarn to the front of the work (as if to purl), and slip one stitch from the left needle to the right (again, as if to purl). Then, turn the work over. The yarn is now again at the back of the piece and the left and right needles have changed places. Bring the yarn to the front, and slip one stitch from the left to the right needle. The wrap and turn is now complete; if the next stitch is a knit stitch, remember to return the yarn to the back of the piece before beginning.

WORK EVEN: Continue knitting without increasing or decreasing.

WS (WRONG SIDE): The inside or non-public side of a sweater. Also stated to indicate which side is facing you when carrying out instructions.

WYIF: With the yarn in the front of the work (toward you).

YARN OVER (YO): Also known as YARN FORWARD. Making a yarn over is a simple way to increase stitches or to make a hole in the knitting, and is popularly combined with a decrease such as knit two together to keep the number of stitches the same across the row. Working a yarn over is the same whether you are knitting or purling the next stitch. When knitting, wrap the yarn around the needle and leave it in the back; when purling, wrap it all the way around the needle so the yarn is back in front where it needs to be to purl. To work a yarn over increase at the beginning of a knit row, bring your yarn to the front of your work and knit the first stitch of the row. To knit that first stitch, you move the yarn from the front to the back over the top of the right needle tip while it is inserted into the first stitch. To work a yarn over increase at the beginning of a purl row, bring your yarn to the back of your work and purl the first stitch of the row. You will bring the yarn from the back to the front over the right needle to purl this first stitch.

SKILL LEVELS

BEGINNER
Projects for first-time knitters using basic knit and purl stitches. Minimal shaping.

EASY
Projects using basic stitches, repetitive stitch patterns, simple color changes, and simple shaping and finishing.

INTERMEDIATE
Projects with a variety of stitches, such as basic cables and lace, simple intarsia, double–pointed needles and knitting in the round needle techniques, mid–level shaping and finishing.

EXPERIENCED
Projects using advanced techniques and stitches, such as short rows, fair isle, more intricate intarsia, cables, lace patterns, and numerous color changes.

YARN WEIGHTS AND SUBSTITUTIONS

YARN WEIGHT SYMBOL	(0)	(1)	(2)	(3)	(4)	(5)	(6)
Type of Yarns in Category	Fingering	Lace, Fingering, Sock	Sport	DK, Light Worsted	Worsted, Aran	Chunky	Bulky, Roving
Knit Gauge Range* in Stockinette Stitch to 4 inches [10 cm]	33–40 sts	27–32 sts	23–26 sts	21–24 sts	16–20 sts	12–15 sts	6–11 sts
Recommended Needle in US Size Range	000–1	1–3	3–5	5–7	7–9	9–11	11 and larger
Recommended Needle in Metric Size Range	1.5–2.25mm	2.25–3.25mm	3.25–3.75mm	3.75–4.5mm	4.5–5.5mm	5.5–8mm	8mm and larger

*GUIDELINES ONLY:
The above chart reflects the most commonly used gauges and needle or hook sizes for specific yarn categories.

SIZING CHART / STANDARD BODY MEASUREMENTS

SIZE	BUST	WAIST	HIPS
XS	28–30	20–22	30–32
S	32–34	24–26	34–36
M	36–38	28–30	38–40
L	40–42	32–34	42–44
1X	44–46	36–38	46–48
2X	48–50	40–42	50–52

RESOURCES

Artyarns
39 Westmoreland Avenue
White Plains, NY 10606
914-428-0333
www.artyarns.com

Berroco Inc.
PO Box 367
14 Elmdale Rd.
Uxbridge, MA 01569
508-278-2527
www.berroco.com

Brown Sheep Company, Inc.
100662 County Road 16
Mitchell, NB 69357
800-826-9136
www.brownsheep.com

Cascade Yarns Inc.
1224 Andover Park E.
Tukwilia, WA 98188
206-574-0440
www.cascadeyarns.com

Estelle Yarns
(for Estelle and Lana Grossa)
2220 Midland Avenue, Unit 65
Scarborough, ON Canada M1P 3E6
800-387-5167
www.estelleyarns.com

Karabella
1201 Broadway
New York, NY 10001
800-550-0898
www.karabellayarns.com

Knit Picks
13118 N.E. 4th Street
Vancouver, WA 98684
800-574-132
www.knitpicks.com

Lion Brand Yarn
135 Kero Road
Carlstadt, NJ 07072
800 258-9276
www.lionbrandyarn.com

Louet Sales
3425 Hands Rd.
Prescott, ON Canada K0E 1T0
613-925-4502
www.louet.com

Malabrigo Yarn
8424 NW 56th St.
Suite 80496, Miami, FL 33166
786-866-6187
www.malabrigoyarn.com

Muench Yarns
(for Lana Grossa)
1323 Scott St.
Petaluma, CA 94954
800-733-9276
www.muenchyarns.com

Needful Yarns
155 Champagne Dr.
Unit 8
Toronto, ON Canada
M3J 2C6 or
60 Industrial Parkway PMB #233
Cheektowaga, NY 14227
866-800-4700
www.needfulyarnsinc.com

Prism Arts Inc.
3140 30th Ave N.
St. Petersburg, FL 33714
727-528-3800
www.prismyarn.com

Tahki • Stacy Charles Inc
70-30 80th St. Bldg #36
Glendale, NY 11385
800-338-9276
www.tahkistacycharles.com

Westminster Fibers
(for Rowan)
165 Ledge St., Nashua, NH 03060
800-445-9276
www.knitrowan.com

INDEX note: page numbers in *italics* indicate patterns.

Published in the United States by Potter Craft, an imprint of the Crown Publishing Group, a division of Random House, Inc., New York.
www.crownpublishing.com
www.pottercraft.com

POTTER CRAFT and colophon is a registered trademark of Random House, Inc.

Portions of this work were originally published in the following:

Big Girl Knits by Jillian Moreno and Amy R. Singer, copyright © 2006 by Quirk Packaging, text copyright © 2008 by Jillian Moreno and Amy R. Singer

Knits Three Ways by Melissa Matthay, copyright © 2007 by Melissa Matthay, photographs by Alan Foreman, photographs copyright © 2007 Alan Foreman

More Big Girl Knits by Jillian Moreno and Amy R. Singer, copyright © 2008 by Jillian Moreno and Amy R. Singer, photographs by Lise Varette, copyright © Lise Varette

Mother-Daughter Knits by Sally Melville and Caddy Melville Ledbetter, copyright © 2009 by Sally Melville and Candace Ledbetter, photographs by Rose Callahan, photographs copyright © Rose Callahan.

Romantic Hand Knits by Annie Modesitt, copyright © 2007 by Annie Modesitt, photographs by Thayer Allyson Gowdy, photographs copyright © 2007 by Thayer Allyson Gowdy

Runway Knits by Berta Karapetyan, copyright © 2007 by Berta Karapetyan, photographs by Justin William Lin, photographs copyright © 2007 by Justin William Lin

Library of Congress Cataloging-in-Publication Data

Knits That Fit : Instructions, Patterns, and Tips for Getting the Right Fit / Edited by Potter Craft. -- First Edition.
        pages cm
Portions of this work were previously published.
ISBN-13: 978-0-307-58666-7 (alk. paper)
ISBN-10: 0-307-58666-9 (alk. paper)
1. Knitting--Patterns. 2. Clothing and dress measurements. I. Potter Craft (Firm)

TT820.K69453 2011
746.43'2--dc222010044435

Printed in China

Design by La Tricia Watford

10 9 8 7 6 5 4 3 2 1

First Edition

Thanks to the Yarn Council of America (www.yarnstandards.com) for their Standard Yarn Weight System chart, which appears on page 173.